# Twin Expectations

# Twin Expectations

## Raising the Bar, Raising Expectations, Raising Children!

Judge Eileen A. Olds

iUniverse, Inc.
Bloomington

**Twin Expectations**
**Raising the Bar, Raising Expectations, Raising Children**

iUniverse books may be ordered through booksellers or by contacting:

iUniverse
1663 Liberty Drive
Bloomington, IN 47403
www.iuniverse.com
1-800-Authors (1-800-288-4677)

Because of the dynamic nature of the Internet, any web addresses or links contained in this book may have changed since publication and may no longer be valid. The views expressed in this work are solely those of the author and do not necessarily reflect the views of the publisher, and the publisher hereby disclaims any responsibility for them.

Cover photo of Kaylee Collins, compliments of her parents, Tony Collins and Karen Cooper-Collins.

ISBN: 978-1-4759-6469-1 (sc)
ISBN: 978-1-4759-6470-7 (hc)
ISBN: 978-1-4759-6471-4 (e)

Library of Congress Control Number: 2012922556

Printed in the United States of America

iUniverse rev. date: 12/17/12

*To Mommie (Puddin') for everything!*

# *Acknowledgments*

To the Almighty Judge who still amazes me with His goodness. To Him, who gave me the desire to write this book while sometimes letting me think that it was my idea! I will serve Him all the days of my life!

To Francine Olds, MD, "Fran," my brilliant and hilarious twin, who is half of most of my inspirations and expectations: my womb mate, best friend since birth, and best constructive critic! I honestly cannot dare to think of what life would have been like without you, "Doog"! You knew I would write this book even if nobody else believed I would get around to it.

To Brett and Bria Harrell, my nephew and niece, who are further proof that it takes a developmental team to raise children. I can't wait to see how your future unfolds. I couldn't love you any more. You really are royalty to me, "Count" and "Countess"!

To Earl C. Robinson, who believes in me and loves me no matter what. Thanks for understanding me for all of these years. For those who ask what we have in common: I love Earl, and Earl loves Earl, LOL! Thanks for always responding, "That's okay, honey." I love you, "Bus"!

To Joan Jeter, my older sister, who witnessed the twin expectations in action. What a gift you got when you were twelve years old. Oh well … love you, "Junny"!

To Judge Belinda Hill, my other "sister," thanks for letting me ramble on and on about my visions for the future and for guarding our friendship with your life!

And to the rest of my Kappa Rho, Delta Sigma Theta Line sisters (along with Fran and Belinda): Carla Harrell, Valerie Lewis, Cleo Powell,

Cassandra Allen, Barbara Moore, and Terry Williams, who became family all those years ago. My sisters! We made it out of UVA and we made it!

To my dear friends Kim, Vennie, Birdie, Bessida, Marilynn, Karen and Pam, Vicki and Valerie Kay, who always show up when I really need them, no matter how long it has been. I have my own story with each of you. You are my gold friends.

To Dolores, Alotha, Lisa, Jesse, Alfreda and Jerrauld who know "the stories"; my sincere gratitude for always listening.

To Faye, Yvette, Schronda, Sonya, Michelle and "San" for checking in on me and not knowing why I was missing sometimes, but still not judging me; and to Joe A who asked, "Where's the book?" not knowing that I was already on it!

To Valda Gibson and Denise Gibson Bailey for raising Bethany, Paul, and Matthew; to my cousin Amanda Patterson-Womble for raising Azel, Adam, and Avery; and to Stephanie Vincent Johnson for raising Morgan, Chase, and Blair. You are all further proof that Puddin's way of parenting still works!

To Rusty, the best editor around, who felt what I was talking about from the beginning and helped keep me grounded while I took this leap of faith! Thanks, Rusty, for understanding "frantic"!

To Aimee, Traci, Sarah, Jan, Mason, and Emily at iUniverse for explaining the hundreds of things I never knew were involved in publishing a book!

To Rev. Michael Toliver for soul-stirring, inspiring sermons!

To the late Judge James M. Walton, and the late Attorney James A. Overton; and to the late Dr. George T. Alston; and to Dr. W. Stanley Jennings, for being early role models in the twin professions.

To Marshawn Evans, for letting me use that phone charger all those years ago and for agreeing that this is not just a book, but a movement!

To Lashawne, Asarene, Shaunna, Allegra, Diane, Kaye, Angela, Frederika, Yashima, and Zoie, "the Mastermind Group."

To my dad, Isaac J. Olds, who always preached "education and good reputation," and to the rest of my family, which is in no way perfect, but perfectly imperfect, I love you all!

And finally to the countless little children who have warmed my heart, whom I have wept for and prayed for, and whom I hope to have encouraged!

# Contents

Acknowledgments     vii

Introduction: "How Come You Never Told Me That?"     xi

1. The Confidence to Make Wise Choices     1
2. Accountability in All Things     15
3. The Power of Purpose     31
4. There Is Freedom in Discipline     43
5. Creating Resilient Children     57
6. Manners Matter     71
7. More Independence Sooner     81
8. Love Your Sister     89
9. Watch Out for the Trucks     101
10. The Endurance Test     107

Epilogue     115

# *Introduction*

## *"How Come You Never Told Me That?"*

THIS IS A BOOK about children, parents, and the choices we make as we raise children in these very uncertain times. Fortunately for me, I had a mother who encouraged the meaningful decisions I made growing up, nurtured every idea, and, above all, fostered hope in our home.

I always felt that I had the most protection imaginable from the best mother in the world. I knew from the beginning that being a mother was what my mom considered to be her biggest accomplishment in life. I only wish more mothers were like her—that more sons and daughters were as fortunate as me and my sisters, Joan and Fran.

It's clear that they are not. As a judge in a Juvenile and Domestic Relations District Court in Virginia, I have a front-row seat to exactly the kinds of long-simmering ills that are affecting this country's families. However, this book is not about what happens in a courtroom, nor is it an exposé on the people who appear there. Instead, it is simply about how love, care, concern, and guiding principles from a devoted mother protected me from many of the dangers outside my door and made a world of a difference.

Every day I see families torn apart not just by poverty, joblessness, or crime—although those are very real contributing factors that none of us can ignore—but also by the increasing disconnect between parent and child.

I am talking about that lack of a basic and undeniable connection that should exist between parent and child that can, and will, affect all of us in the long run—that guarded and trusted role that starts at home, one-on-one, between parent and child. If every parent raised a healthy child in a healthy home with a healthy relationship, the world would be a much brighter, safer, more harmonious place!

I firmly believe that. Don't you?

I can't speak expertly to strategies for economic recovery, to complexities of the real-estate market, or to the nuances of medical procedures, but what I can speak to with authority *and* experience are the ingredients of the relationship between parent and child, which I proudly benefited from, or the lack thereof, which I witness day in and day out.

Although sometimes necessary, it is not easy to take a child away from his or her parents, whether it's because that child has committed a crime or because the parents are no longer fit to raise that child; yet it happens in courtrooms across the country every day. I believe that our country faces a grave future indeed if we continue to solve our family problems and resolve our family disputes by default or through court orders and institutional solutions rather than through strong familial support, early intervention, and good, old-fashioned education. Honestly, I see no other remedy until parents and other entrusted caregivers begin accepting responsibility for their own actions inside and outside the home.

The fact is, children can't *do better* until they *know better*. I regularly see children who, for perhaps the very first time in their lives, are hearing that *what they've done is wrong*. I see children who are about to receive meaningful consequences for their actions for the first time.

I watch children who are finally being told that they can't just take what they want, or go to school only when they feel like it, or terrorize a teacher or fellow classmate or strangers just because they can. I have witnessed children who truly have not been required to consistently follow rules and children who have not been told that they cannot do everything they want to do and that "everybody is doing it" doesn't mean that something is right. Very few parents would disagree with the concept of imposing and reinforcing boundaries, but in practice, the concept appears to elude them. I can almost see the children looking up at their parents as if to say, "How come *you* never told me that?"

Oftentimes, the parents seem as if they are hearing it for the first time as well. I think to myself that it's no wonder the child has a warped set of values and a marked disconnect between behavior and consequences.

In many cases, there is no need to look any further than at the parents who have produced a negative mirror image of themselves in their children. Very few parents, to say nothing of the children, set about to do wrong in a purposeful, malignant way; most of them simply go wrong for lack of any better direction—or better parenting. Many times the transgressions are generational. We can see history repeating itself, year after year, child after child, simply because no one puts on the brakes and says, "This is wrong. Stop doing that," and most importantly, "I expect more from you, so you should expect more from yourself."

I am by no means suggesting that parents can always be held directly responsible for the actions of their children. However, many households become breeding grounds for an overall sense of irresponsibility and lack of accountability. Many parents have simply abdicated their duties to their children.

When parents are not there, or the children are not there, or even when families are home together and they're *still* not connecting, it is difficult to share lessons, impart values, or form bonds.

And yet who am I to say that the parents raising children today were ever really "raised" themselves? In a very real sense, there are many examples of children raising children. I see grandparents raising grandchildren. I see troubled parents, confused parents, hopeless parents, frustrated parents, and oftentimes neglectful parents—not always in a physical sense perhaps, but in an emotional sense.

And these are the adults! If we can't keep it together for our kids, how can we ever expect the kids to keep it together for themselves? I *am* well aware of the fact—more so than most, given my proximity to disturbed, scared, anxious, and dysfunctional families on a daily basis—that there is something very wrong with the way we are raising our children these days, not only individually as parents but collectively as extended family, as a community, and as a nation.

That's why I felt compelled to write this book. I know what it's like to come from a home where children were valued, cherished, and above all expected to achieve. My twin sister Francine Olds, MD, a noted gynecologist in the medical community, and I were raised by a single mother who genuinely and frequently imparted life lessons and high expectations.

Yes, my twin and I are a doctor and a judge, yet we weren't raised in some elite, upper-crust Ivy League family. There are no other doctors or lawyers in our family. We didn't come from a lineage of lots of money or grow up with overflowing resources. My mother worked hard as a teacher and she did the best she could to raise three girls on her own, without any immediate family near us. We were raised, like so many children I see every day, in a single-parent household, but it never felt like we were missing anything or deprived because of outstanding parental guidance. Yes! We were raised by a single parent, a divorced mother, who worked full- time outside the home!

But those words had a lot more drama attached to them back then. When my parents divorced, the divorce rate was not at nearly 50 percent, as it is today, so my mother had to deal with the additional stigma of being a frowned upon, nontraditional woman. There were many societal ills, complicated situations, family shame, and social demons right in my own family, but so what!

If society had had its way, neither of us girls may have succeeded, let alone risen to the top of our professions in such highly competitive fields. Raised by our single mother to defy expectations rather than succumb to them, my twin sister and I were taught to follow our own paths, not those predestined by the culture or time we grew up in.

Today when people meet me and my sister and hear of our "twin" accomplishments, their first reaction is to ask, "What did your mama do?!"

My pat answer subsequently became the title of this book: "She had 'twin expectations,' that's what!" In other words, my mother *expected* us to meet society's positive expectations *and* hers. She expected us to go far. And she expected us to do well in school and stay out of trouble. She made every effort to rescue us from negative influences while fostering the positive.

So many of the families I see and interact with at educational or community events expect so little of themselves, to say nothing of their children. It's as if they as a family, and we as a culture, have given up on our kids, on their future, and, in the process, on our future as well.

That's why this book, *Twin Expectations*, is a hope-filled guide for reclaiming what matters most—our children. It is absolutely necessary that we raise the bar and raise expectations in raising children. I believe that my perspective from the bench and beyond provides a long-awaited, fresh vision for our communities and country. I know that there is something to what my mother did!

*Fran, Joan, and me with Mom*

# Chapter 1

# The **Confidence** to Make Wise Choices

To lead or to follow.
To stay in class or skip school.
To stay in school or drop out.
To pay for that bracelet or steal it.
To do drugs or just walk away.
To fight or take the high road.
Our children make choices every day, but are they *wise choices*?

Too often, and for all the wrong reasons, kids make the wrong choices. Whether out of impulse, peer pressure, or simply a lack of tools to guide them, the choices kids make now can temporarily or even permanently affect their future. I can honestly say that I have never been in a fistfight. However, I have taken on many mental, emotional, and character fights! I think part of the reason I never got in a fistfight is because my mom always emphasized "taking the high road" and insisted that we weigh how momentary fits of rage could affect our standing among our peers, teachers, and neighbors (literally and figuratively), not to mention that fighting was not ladylike. I can still hear her saying, "Just walk away!"

Every day kids end up suffering the consequences of the choices that they have made. Too few of them understand that what they chose to do could land them in hot water or hurt someone. Sadly, too few care about the consequences of their negative behavior because they have not been taught to care about them.

That's why it's up to us as role models, parents, and people who care to help them make sound choices. But how? One of the greatest gifts we can give our children is the confidence to make wise choices. My mom exuded confidence, and she made it look so easy.

Part of teaching the art of confidence is simply leading by example through making good choices of our own, and equally important is helping kids understand the consequences of both good and bad choices. Puddin'(the family nickname that we often called my mother)would remind us to be confident in our decisions, and then "hold your head high," she would say.

## THE NINE GIFTS OF CONFIDENCE

To help see the true power of confidence and how it might affect your child's decision-making process, here are what I consider the_Nine Gifts of Confidence:

### The First Gift of Confidence: *Security*

When your child feels confident, he or she also feels secure in who he or she is. When a child feels secure, he or she also has more confidence. I can't stress enough how important security is toward helping a child become a healthy, vibrant adult.

When your child is secure in who he or she is, what his or her strengths and weaknesses are, and what he or she is all about, he or she naturally finds it much easier to

- make wise choices;
- say no to unwise choices;
- lead instead of follow;
- follow the right person, if he or she must follow at all; and
- choose his or her own path, regardless of popularity or peer pressure.

The insecure child, on the other hand, finds it nearly impossible to make wise choices because he or she has no idea who he or she is, what he or she stands for, or, in many cases, what's right or wrong.

### The Second Gift of Confidence: *Poise*

When my twin sister and I were growing up, we were often struck by our mother's poise in the midst of hard decisions, tough times, or even major life decisions. While she was no emotionless cyborg, our mother personified grace under fire.

Today, however, I often see mothers as emotional and tantrum prone as their children. Children are like sponges, soaking up the mood, tone, and atmosphere of home. If they are raised by excitable parents, children often become excitable themselves.

In my experience, excitable children are often too emotional or even too frantic to make wise choices, while a child filled with poise, who can exhibit grace under pressure, can make wiser choices from a place of calm.

### The Third Gift of Confidence: *Calm*

A sense of calm is so important for today's child. While childlike behavior includes a degree of impatience, anxiety, and selfishness, I'm amazed by the number of children who can't be still, stay quiet while others are speaking, or mind their parents even with constant redirection. I can only imagine how they act in a classroom or at home.

But the confident child can go through life with a sense of calm about him or her, making it easier for him or her to approach choices more calmly, if not more wisely.

I find that many children make choices rashly, in an environment of excitability, the very opposite of calm. I'm often struck by the thought that if that child could simply find some peace and more stability in his or her life, he or she could ultimately make better choices.

### The Fourth Gift of Confidence: *Trust*

Specifically, the fourth gift of confidence refers to trusting oneself. One of the hardest parts of parenting is to allow our children to grow, to learn, and to test their wings and fly—or fall—on their own.

But how can our children learn to trust themselves if we can't learn to trust *them*? As I move through these gifts of confidence, I am reminded again and again of how integral the parents' role is in building a strong sense of confidence—not overconfidence, but sincere, genuine, and authentic self-confidence—in their children.

My mother often reminded us that no one was any better than we were. On the other hand, if we got haughty at all, she also reminded us that we were *no better* than anyone else either. She taught us to be mindful of the delicate balance between confidence and conceit. Confidence was admired, conceit was not, and trusting ourselves was bolstered by that confidence.

Children should be told often what their individual strengths are and reminded that they are equipped to make wise choices. They should, in addition, be rewarded for maintaining the trust that we have in them and that we instill in them. Simply communicate with them, one-on-one, as often as possible. Talk to them about their fears, their accomplishments, their doubts, their strengths, and their weaknesses. Validate their worth as trustworthy individuals.

You don't have to be your child's incessant cheerleader, rooting him or her on for even the slightest tiny thing, but taking the time to check the pulse of your child's enthusiasm for this or that endeavor is a great way to show him or her that not only do you care, but that he or she is worth caring about. Your demonstration of trust in your child's decision-making is more important and has more impact than any peer's opinion ever could. Trust your child to trust himself or herself.

*Fran and Me at two and a half years olds*

## The Fifth Gift of Confidence: *Establishing Priorities*

I've seen too many insecure children who also lack confidence come into the courtroom for everything from minor infractions to major, even violent, crimes. The more I dig into their individual backgrounds, the more I discover how skewed their priorities often are.

I am convinced that if parents can isolate and identify their children's priorities, they can usually see the warning signs of misplaced priorities long before their children are in trouble. It's difficult for children to hide what they make important in their lives.

You can walk into a child's room and see what's important to him or her, from the posters on the wall, to his or her choice of music, to his or her list of Facebook friends.

And in case you are wondering, let me just say it: it is absurd for any child under eighteen years old to have a Facebook, Twitter, or any social media account without the parent taking regular peeps into the social-networking associations the child has established.

Trust me, this is *not* an invasion of your child's privacy. You are the parent; he or she is the child! (I have to keep saying it because sometimes I think we all forget that.)

The fact is, in your house, under your rules, your child should have no expectation of privacy when it comes to your overarching concern for his or her safety. A review of the source of your child's interactions paints a clear picture as to what his or her priorities are. The priorities that children set are moving and driving forces in their attitudes, morals, and behaviors.

To pinpoint your child's priorities, or to at least begin the process, ask yourself:

**Who is my child making a priority?** For instance, is there suddenly a new friend in his or her life? A new name you keep hearing as he or she talks on the telephone or communicates via text or Facebook?

**What is my child making a priority?** Is he or she suddenly into sports, or skateboarding, or hanging around on the corner? Has something or someone suddenly appeared in his or her life that is causing you concern?

**How often is my child making something or someone a priority?** There are priorities and then there are distractions.

Fall and a new school year can mean new priorities for kids, like sports or extracurricular activities, but hopefully not distractions. Oftentimes unhealthy priorities border on and even quickly become unhealthy distractions.

**Why is my child making this a priority?** Again, look beyond the obvious and dig deeper. If your child is suddenly glued to the computer, it doesn't necessarily have to be a bad thing. Maybe he or she is working on a book report that's due next week or taking advantage of some new online opportunities for extra credit that the school is offering.

**Is my child hiding his or her priorities from me?** It does become a challenge when children start to hide their priorities from their parents. With today's modern schedules, working parents, extracurricular activities, and other family demands, it's often hard to keep tabs on your child at all times. However, more often than not, a few simple questions can reveal what your child's priorities are and why. Sometimes we have to force ourselves to ask them. But asking the right questions reinforces the need for the child to align with positive priorities, or at least distinguish from the poor or less important ones! Again, clear, positive priorities equal more confidence in the direction your future teacher, scientist, Broadway star, doctor, or judge takes.

**The Sixth Gift of Confidence:** *Self-Assurance*

To be self-assured is to trust in your own abilities, your own path, your own choices, and your own strengths and weaknesses. While few of us are ever completely self-assured, even in adulthood, the sooner a child can learn to validate the decisions that he or she makes, the sooner he or she will begin making the right choices. Your child also needs to look to you for confirmation when he or she makes intelligent, well-reasoned decisions.

One of the reasons kids make bad choices is because they're uncertain. Not only does confidence begin to erase that uncertainty with each passing day, but being self-assured makes one more certain of what is right or wrong.

**The Seventh Gift of Confidence:** *Leadership*

I see far too many followers and nowhere near enough leaders. But what happens to insecure children is that when they don't find guidance and intrafamily leadership at home, they look for it outside the home.

Usually they find it in their friends. If their friends are immature or insecure themselves or are really misguided parasites or users, they are going to be following the wrong leaders and head straight down the wrong path. The greatest leaders a child has are his or her parents. Lead the way.

**The Eighth Gift of Confidence:** *Respect for Authority*

Confident children aren't threatened by authority; therefore, they find it much easier to respect authority. Part of childhood is learning to know who to listen to and who to filter out.

Too often insecure children respect the wrong type of authority: bullies, thugs, dropouts, and other troublemakers. Being confident in who they are allows children to tell the difference between not just wise and unwise choices but also between the right and wrong kinds of authority. My mom taught us and demanded that we respect adults as a higher authority. We were expected to pay attention when adults were speaking, to give up our seats to those older than we, to hold the door open for them, to say "Yes, ma'am," or "Yes, sir," and so on. Back talking was not allowed.

Mom, Fran, and I often fondly recalled a time that one of Mom's coworkers was riding in the car with us. She constantly talked about how great she was, how great her son was, what material possessions they had, and on and on. Fran and I, only seven years old, were in the backseat about to burst with laughter and seriously wanting her to shut up but sucked it in. As soon as we dropped her off at her residence, we erupted in laughter, cackling and declaring that "She was bragging!" but we didn't dare disrespect the lady or comment in her presence, and we knew that we better not! Puddin' had no tolerance for disrespect for authority. "Be nice," especially to adults, was a frequent refrain.

It is well known that one of the reasons that gang affiliation is so deeply entrenched in our society is because of the respect for the hierarchy and authority within the organization. A high level of secrecy in gangs is dominant. The indoctrination and subsequent acts are in large part a demonstration of the respect for the authority that rules within the gang set.

Again, if the authority and direction does not come consistently from one who has been fostering the child's best interest at heart, the clues and directions will come from those who are ill-equipped to guide them.

### The Ninth Gift of Confidence: *Accomplishment*

I've found that confident kids are also achievers. They set goals, they reach them, they accomplish what they set out to do, and they are proud of their accomplishments. So are their parents, who are generally involved in both supervising and celebrating those accomplishments.

In my experience, celebrating any accomplishment your child achieves is not only a good way to build confidence, but also a great way to build a stronger relationship in general and demonstrate pride in the child's accomplishments. I firmly believe that the dollar per A that Puddin' gave us for good report cards served as a great incentive to make those As a pattern that lasted throughout our scholastic years.

## CELEBRATE CONFIDENCE, NOT CONFLICT

Confidence comes from a place of security, poise, calm, and trust—the child's trust in self, and the trust placed in that child. We build their confidence when we let our children know that they are self-sufficient, worthy, and capable. The goal is to eventually let them stand on their own two feet, and confidence is one of the best tools we can give them to help them do just that.

When I was growing up, there was never a rational idea I had, a notion I was considering, or a risk I was willing to take that my mother wasn't willing to support or take with me!

If I came home from school and said, "Mom, I'm thinking about running for student body president," her immediate, loud, and instinctive response would be, "Good for you! Go for it!"

If my sister said, "Mom, I am going to find a cure for cancer someday," she would have burst into shouts of joy and promoted the idea that she could do it!

Puddin' never encouraged us to be foolhardy, of course, but she understood that kids have to take risks and learn to grow. As much as it is our job to protect them, we must also prepare our children for the very unfair, very real world they will one day grow up to inhabit.

Our mother knew that—win or lose—the trials and tribulations of running for student government, for example, would prepare me for life, just as she knew that my sister may or may not grow out of her desire to find a much-needed cure for disease. Either way, she supported our decisions because she wanted us to be independent, to be self-sufficient, to be secure in our own decisions, to be confident, and above all, to continue to dream.

The fact is that we often do a disservice to our children by focusing on what they can't do rather than what they can. We simply do not celebrate the accomplishments our children make: mediocre, good, great, or anywhere in between.

In fact, we do quite the opposite. Rather than celebrating or paying attention to the good that our children do, we are frequently only aroused when they have done something bad.

So many children continue to act out in a negative manner because the celebrations in their lives center around negative behavior. The parent who only shows up to school when the child is suspended but not to the PTA meeting or for parent-teacher conferences is showing the child more attention and having more contact with school than he or she does when there is not trouble at hand. Likewise, the parent who joins with the child (without proper exploration or validation) in asserting that "it's the teacher's fault" tacitly ratifies the child's misbehavior.

The message the child soon gets is that *the parent is more responsive to bad than good*. Likewise, the parent who makes every hour of visitation at the detention home may be the same parent who never spent one hour of exclusive contact with the child when at home. Suddenly, a child who has been emotionally abandoned for most of his or her life is getting the attention he or she so craved growing up.

I cannot count the times that as a child is led away to start a period of detention, a parent boldly asks, "May I give my child a hug?" My gut reaction is to ask, "A hug? I wonder when the last time was that you hugged your child," I suspect that those hugs may not have been given on a regular basis.

## To Thine Own Self Be True

My mother taught English for more than thirty years and was quite fond of reminding us of Shakespeare's line from his famous play *Hamlet*—"To thine own self be true." For her children, this meant that we should not only trust our beliefs and instincts but also follow them.

I believe that many children lack a true sense of self; they really don't know themselves. They also get conflicting messages from the adults in their lives. You can't do this, you can't do that, you can't go here, you can't go there. They start to wonder, "Well, what can I do? Where can I go?"

Lots of them don't even want to be themselves; they'd rather be basketball players or movie stars or rappers or dancers in a hip-hop video. Many watch their favorite reality TV stars and want to be famous simply for the sake of being famous.

As a result, kids who don't know themselves simply can't be true to themselves. They don't lead, they follow; they don't decide, they give in. But confidence can help them make better decisions, choose better friends, and even get better grades.

As Puddin' would say, you don't have to be perfect, but you have to do your best, because "that's all the Good Lord requires." To me and my sister, this basically afforded us a blank slate. As long as we tried our best and gave it our all, we could literally do and be anything.

That mind-set gave us the confidence to try new things, to take risks, and to embrace failure as long as it taught us valuable life lessons. In many ways, I think Fran and I grew acclimated to challenge. We got a thrill from succeeding but also from pushing ourselves just a little harder the next time, even if it meant failure.

Kids these days seem so afraid of failing, they rarely try anything. They hang with the same friends because it's comfortable; a new set of friends might reject them. They stay on the same path even when they could be so much more.

Rumors play a decided role in success or failure. You know the rumor that invariably surrounds every kid: he or she is cool, a geek, a nerd, a jock, a tramp, a brain, or on the wrong track. Unfortunately, as parents, adults, counselors, and teachers, whatever role we have in a child's life, we're often guilty of starting the rumor.

Bad rumors can cheapen our children and make them less than what they really are, or guide them on a path they never should have taken in the first place.

After all, if you're told again and again you can't do something, you will believe that you can't. Parents who propose that "He's not cut out for that," or "That's not her!" are setting their children up for failure. If a child hears that, he or she will believe it. And that's how kids start to lose their confidence—because of the impression that they'll never succeed. No matter how hard they try, they simply cannot succeed because they believe they're not cut out for it. I can't ever imagine my mother telling me, "You can't do that."

Labels are so important to children. It begins early. Good labels encourage. If the first-grade teacher says that you're smart, you're going to be promoted to the "smart" second-grade class, then the smart third-grade class, and so on. Now, you may not be smart at all; you might just be cute, quiet, and well-behaved, and sometimes that's all it takes, all other things being equal.

Positive labels can also be powerful in predicting future success as well. I so vividly recall my second-grade teacher, Dr. Mary Corprew, commenting, "One day you will make a great lawyer!" She said that to me because I had a gift of gab and talked quite a lot for a second grader. Imagine if instead she had said, "Eileen, one day your big mouth is going to get you in big trouble," or "You are a blabbermouth." Thankfully, she viewed what some would have made a negative into a positive and into a powerful projection and satisfying motivation.

And she was right, at least about the lawyer part!

On the other hand, if a child is labeled "slow" or "unmotivated" early on, he or she will carry that presumption with him or her and have a more difficult time overcoming that "slow" track throughout his or her schooling. That's the case even if he or she is gifted but not good at testing or playing by the rules. The label does just that—it labels.

Avoid labels whenever you can, as sometimes even good ones can be limiting if misused. Instead, share with your child the good news that he or she truly can be anything he or she wants to be.

## PARTING WORDS ABOUT THE GIFT OF CONFIDENCE

Make no mistake: *Confidence is a gift that we must give our children.* It is a suit of armor they can wear against the very harsh, very real, very persistent daily challenges of growing up in today's world.

You can't be with them every hour of every day. In fact, with school, work, extracurricular activities, and the challenges of modern family life, you are often away from your kids far more than you are with them.

So who is raising them when you're not? Their teachers, counselors, coaches, babysitters, and neighbors as well. But many of our children are also being raised by the streets, which includes friends and peers who may have no interest in your child whatsoever other than to fulfill their own needs.

Confidence comes in handy when your child is forced to make any one of the hundreds of daily decisions that affect him or her—and you—every day. When your child can stand up for himself or herself, believe in himself or herself, and above all trust himself or herself, your child will have the first tool he or she needs to protect himself or herself when you're not there to protect him or her.

*Graduation from Liberty Park Nursery School*

## BENCHMARKS OF CONFIDENCE

- One of the greatest gifts we can give our children is self-confidence. The other is the freedom to use it wisely.
- Confidence begins at home. No one wants his or her child to be overly confident, but feeling insecure is just as harmful. Lead by example and show your child that confident parents raise confident kids.
- Confidence begins when we teach our children to trust themselves, which likewise begins when *we* begin to trust *them*.
- You can't teach confidence if you don't feel confident yourself. So how confident are you?

# Chapter 2

## *Accountability* in All Things

ABOVE ALL ELSE, MY mother instilled in my sisters and me a fierce independent streak. She made it clear that we could do anything when we set our minds to it, as long as we put action behind our dreams. When I think of how she demonstrated that independence, I think of the saying, "I can show you better than I can tell you." Seeing her as a role model made displays of confidence instinctive.

This is not to say that we raised ourselves—far from it. Mom was always there for us, eager to lend a helping hand, and showing us every step of the way that we really could do it. But her first instinct when it came to teaching was to have us *do it for ourselves* rather than her *doing it for us*.

Naturally, as little girls, we'd come home and want help with our homework, a book report or special project, a spelling test, whatever it was—not because we couldn't do it for ourselves, but because it was just plain easier to have Mom do it for us. And we had the best help of all standing ready: a teacher with a snack of Nabs or Hostess Twinkies waiting at the kitchen counter.

But Mom taught us, much as she taught her students, to try to find the answer *for yourself* before asking for help. After a while, we knew this would be her response, and because the answers were generally found readily, we skipped the whole song and dance of asking the same questions and getting the same answers every day and simply did the work ourselves. Soon it came naturally. We did our schoolwork without much prodding and with a sense of self-pride. Doing it also strengthened our accountability to ourselves for scholastic success!

I can't stress enough what this one lesson has done for my sisters and me. Rather than looking to blame others for our shortcomings or seeking help from outside before looking inside first, we each learned to stand on our own two feet.

The saying, "If at first you don't succeed, try, try again," was engrained into our heads deeply and early. As I grew older, my mother would often remind me that I seemed to never take no for an answer. She would say that with both amazement and pride, but I knew that I became that way because of her direct and indirect teaching.

Her lessons helped us have confidence and faith in ourselves when times got tough. When we looked to ourselves first, we solved more problems more quickly than waiting for others to come to our rescue or find a solution. And when the solution did not come, we tried again. Again, we were accountable for our actions. Sadly, I see a lot of children who become dependent from an early age on everyone *but* themselves.

That scares me sometimes, because there are so many challenges facing our children today, more than ever before. I just hate to see children unprepared for those challenges, looking for help from the outside when they should be looking for ways within themselves to solve those problems.

It's not wrong to get help; Lord knows we all need it from time to time. We all make mistakes and poor decisions, even as grown-ups, but the lesson is in learning and growing from them, not using them as excuses to avoid accountability or to put the blame on others.

Sometimes I'm afraid we're teaching our children to stand in the rain and wait for someone to give them an umbrella rather than simply to bring their own, to run indoors at the first drop, or to even watch the Weather Channel before stepping outside in the first place!

Personal accountability is one of the single most important gifts you can give a child. Much like confidence, it is the gift that keeps on giving because it turns accountable children into accountable adults.

It's incremental—a child who is accountable for his or her own actions becomes a young adult who is accountable for his or her actions, then a college student who is responsible for his or her actions, and finally an adult who is responsible for his or her actions. That's because when we are accountable for what we do, most of the time we only have ourselves to blame.

## "That's Not My Station!"

Have you ever sat in a restaurant with an empty cup of coffee and, after waiting patiently for a refill, asked the next passing waiter for a little more?

Chances are, unless you just happen to ask the restaurant's go-to go-getter, you'll hear some variation of, "That's not my station!" as the waiter rushes by to pour a perfectly good cup of coffee out of the perfectly full pot in his or her station!

I know waiting tables is hard, and one waiter can't hold down the entire fort by himself or herself. But if you've got the pot, and you're standing there rationalizing with a customer, it would actually take less time to simply pour the cup of coffee before moving on back to your own station.

But it's an accountability issue; that one waiter isn't technically assigned to that table, and so it's not his or her responsibility, period. This example demonstrates how some people will not stretch themselves or take on any responsibility that will make them more accountable than they absolutely have to be. It's a generalization, of course, and there are good and bad waiters and good and bad kids and good and bad—well, everybody and everything. But we can't deny the fact that the world is turning into a place where a lot of people simply can't be bothered to be held accountable and responsible.

When children see grown-ups walking away from their responsibilities—be it in a restaurant or on the news—they are given the clear message that "It's okay; it's not your responsibility."

It sounds like such a simple thing, pouring a cup of coffee or not pouring a cup of coffee, but it's indicative of a bigger problem at large.

## Accountability Counts: *Seven Secrets for Making Your Child More Accountable*

Who are your children accountable to? You? Their teachers? Their friends? Themselves? Too many children aren't held accountable for their actions, which makes them feel as if they can do whatever they choose and when things go wrong they can blame it on something or someone else.

Remember, we won't always be around to shoulder the blame, hold their hands, or get them out of trouble. I see kids all the time who've gotten away with too much for too long and aren't properly held accountable until it's too late! To give our children the tools they need to survive, let alone thrive in today's society, we need to hold them accountable for their own actions.

Here are seven secrets for helping your child do just that:

### The First Secret of Accountability: *Independence*

It's okay to let your child exercise his or her independence. In fact, the more independence your child has, the more he or she will *want* to be independent.

Now, being independent is different from simply being alone. Our children are often alone, but frequently dependent. They're dependent on us for their after-school snacks whether we're there or not. They're dependent on us for their lunches, dinners, laundry, housekeeping, and a host of items and chores that probably get you up early in the morning and keep you up late at night.

It's fine to assume all responsibility when children are physically and developmentally unable to contribute, but with age must come independence. Allow your child do those things that are both age appropriate and independence building. "Spoon-feeding," as Puddin' called it, is not the best practice when the child is capable himself or herself. I'll never forget the time that I was preparing a surprise meal for my mom. In the kitchen cabinet, I ran across a canister of bouillon cubes. I saw that the label read "Makes a delicious drink," so I proceeded to do just that. Little did I realize that it actually said "Makes a delicious *hot* drink." Mom, in her most gracious way, assured me that the dinner was delicious, and I think she may have even suffered through drinking a little of the ice-cold bouillon, but then she explained the importance of reading the labels carefully. This is a rite of passage that I humorously recall today. I still read labels very carefully! Taking steps toward independence is encouraged even though mistakes and mishaps are bound to happen along the way. Do you have to be there to greet your child's bus even though you can see him or her get off through your kitchen window? Can you help him or her grow more independent by letting him or her stand at the bus stop alone in the morning (of course watching from the window) even if it's hard at first?

I'm not suggesting you put your child in harm's way or take unnecessary risks, but that's exactly what you're doing by creating a child who is too dependent on you for his or her own good.

Dependence is certainly a handicap as children get older. The more dependent a child is, the less accountable he or she is for his or her own actions because he or she is used to having things done for him or her. The more children do for themselves, the more independent they are and the more accountable they become with each passing day. Whether it is making a bad meal or adding bleach to a load of colored clothing, it is only through the exercise of independent acts that children learn life lessons and become more accountable.

Something as simple as making their own lunch or snack, walking to their school or bus stop alone, or doing their own homework or science fair project without entirely leaning on Mom or Dad can help children grow by leaps and bounds.

**The Second Secret of Accountability:** *Responsibility*

What exactly is your child responsible for in any given day? Is your child responsible for

- chores?
- homework?
- an after-school job?
- sports?
- extracurricular activities?

I'm serious; make a list. You might be surprised by how much you do for your child, or help him or her do, or simply don't expect him or her to do in the first place. It's easy to miss unless you write it down and see it in black and white with your own eyes.

One of the simplest ways to help kids grow in accountability is to give them additional responsibilities with age and/or maturity. Here are some simple responsibilities you can give your child that won't tax him or her too much but will help him or her grow into a productive, accountable young adult:

**Snack time/mealtime:** Can your child make his or her own snacks? Does he or she do so? Simple kitchen tasks like spreading peanut butter on a slice of bread, helping with dinner, or even setting the table can help teach a child responsibility and make him or her accountable for at least some of his or her own meals. As with most things, there is a preferred window of opportunity. When it passes, it is much more difficult to break through. Children who never learn to prepare a lunch are the ones who become adults who do not know how to prepare a meal.

**Pet power:** If you have a pet, this is a great, low-impact way to help your child take on more responsibility. If you make taking care of the pet a condition to receiving a pet, follow-through is absolutely necessary. Have your child clean out the litter box, walk the dog, or feed the fish, the parrot, or the turtle. If you don't have a pet but still want to teach your child some responsibility, get him or her a goldfish. If pets are just not in the lineup, at least have your child water the plants and flowers. It could be the first step toward a much more accountable child.

**Daily chores:** We had chores growing up—nothing unreasonable or too terribly taxing (although it often felt that way at the time), but enough to make it clear that we weren't going to escape our share of responsibility in my mother's house. Most of the time, it never felt like a chore since it was routine, expected, introduced incrementally, and my sisters and I considered it a natural way of life. You combed your hair, took a shower, had your breakfast, emptied the trash, cleared the table, and unpacked the groceries; they all fell in the same category of simply living our lives. Having daily chores early on helped prepare us for the rigors of schoolwork, college, and life in general. It helped us with so many life issues that, sadly, I see kids struggling with today, such as completing assignments, managing time, meeting goals, and reaching deadlines.

**Homework:** You would think it would be a no-brainer that homework is a child's responsibility, but you may be surprised. In many households, homework is either neglected, delayed, forgotten, ignored, or, even worse, simply not a priority. To the contrary, there are households where the adults do the homework consistently, not the child. Many times children don't take the importance seriously, and parents refuse to enforce consistently until it's too late, grades slip, failure is threatening, and suddenly it's a mad dash to catch up. But homework is every student's responsibility. It is also a parental responsibility to set proper boundaries as to when and how homework is prioritized. In fact, one of the main reasons why teachers assign homework in the first place is to hold children *accountable for their own education.*

## The Third Secret of Accountability: *Fellowship*

How much time do your children spend outside the home aside from going to school? Are they involved in church groups, sports teams, extracurricular activities, clubs, or organizations?

Statistically speaking, most juvenile delinquency occurs between the time school lets out for the day and dinnertime. Between three thirty and six thirty in the evening, there is a significant spike in bad behavior—not at midnight, not during the dead of night, although that certainly happens, but in the middle of the afternoon and evening, right under everyone's noses. That is, if anyone is looking at all.

That's why so many churches and community organizations offer after-school programs; they're trying to fill those three hours with productive, supervised activities instead of leaving the kids to the unproductive, unsupervised streets. In large part, juvenile delinquency occurs because there is nothing preplanned to do. In many respects, it is not surprising when a juvenile responds, "I don't know," when asked how or why he or she participated in unacceptable behavior.

Active, engaging, and positive fellowship with peers their own age in controlled environments helps children become more independent from the home and, as a result, more accountable for their own actions.

Churches not only teach spiritual lessons but lessons in responsibility, citizenship, community, and accountability as well. Clubs like the Girl Scouts, Boy Scouts, Boys and Girls Clubs, and the YMCA have programs that hold children accountable for their actions, behavior, and goals they've set for themselves. Sports participation also helps a child become accountable; he or she must bring his or her own uniform, show up to practice and games on time, and be an asset to the team on and off the playing field.

Encourage your child to participate more, not less. My mother had a saying: "Idle hands are the devil's workshop." She meant that with little to do and nowhere to go, children often get into trouble. Idle, unsupervised kids with nothing better to do than roam the streets will naturally have more opportunities to hang with and meet unsavory characters who may influence them to do negative things. One of my favorite ongoing activities as a pre-teen was participation in *Jack and Jill of America, Inc.* We had activities that were planned at least monthly with other children from across our city and local area. My mother was a charter member of the Chesapeake, VA Chapter and remained active with us until we finished high school. The fact that the parents socialized alongside the children allowed for a wide network of fun and lasting friendships.

Children who are involved, who participate, and who are held accountable for their own actions will have stronger defenses against negative peer influences and will simply get into less trouble. Fellowship with peers, old friends, and new friends is a great opportunity for participation and growth.

Here are five wonderful venues for fellowship that exist for every family:

**Clubs:** There are so many great, valuable, energetic, and passionate youth groups out there just waiting for your child to join, such as the Boy Scouts, Girl Scouts, Junior Achievement, YMCA, and YWCA. Encourage your child to participate and watch him or her grow into his or her own accountability. Organizations help children learn from responsible club leaders but also from their peer group. Clubs and organizations are also a great way to introduce your child to friends and responsibilities that don't exist at home or school. It will open up a whole new world to explore, learn from, and be challenged by.

**Sports:** Your child doesn't have to be a three-hundred-pound linebacker or six-foot-tall future WNBA star to reap the benefits of organized sports. Nowadays, there is a sport for nearly every child on this planet!

**Church:** Regardless of your religious beliefs, church groups offer a wonderful opportunity for children to gather together in fellowship and experience each other's diverse backgrounds.

Oftentimes you don't even have to be a member of a church to reap the benefits of their youth programs. Churches often provide after-school tutoring, exercise, and esteem-building programs as well.

**School groups:** When I was in school, my mother encouraged my idea of running for student office. I can still recite part of the campaign speech I gave to my junior high school class, remember the outfit I was wearing, and some of what my campaign manager Fran said when she introduced me to the assembly. It was such a rich and rewarding experience for me. I encourage children to join a school group that interests them. Whether it is working in the student government or on the yearbook staff or joining the chess club, the benefits from the relationships your child forms could last them a lifetime. Don't let your child get away with saying he or she is not interested in any of it. Every child has some interest or group with which he or she can identify. To this day, my tenth-grade English teacher, Carole Gibson Flemming, remains a favorite, primarily as an outgrowth of her work in class that extended to the Thespian Society and our involvement in her school theatrical productions. Another bonus of extracurricular school activities is developing closer-knit relationships with peers who don't necessarily go to the same school or whom your child does not normally associate with. It also fosters a closer, hopefully positive relationship between your child and the adult overseers, coaches, sponsors, and others he or she interacts with on a daily basis.

**Community service/charity:** Are you and your child active in your local community? Could you be more active, more giving, of your time? My mom lived by the scripture, "It is more blessed to give than to receive." She gave to individuals whom she knew, but also to those whom she didn't know, through causes and charitable organizations. My mom has more address labels from every organization imaginable and more lightbulbs from the Fire Department Benevolent Association sale than just about anybody else on this earth! In addition to financial charitable contributions, I also recall and value her teaching of community service. I can still see my mother going door-to-door in the neighborhood collecting for Easter Seals, the Muscular Dystrophy Association, or the American Heart Association. The solicitations are still coming in all these years later. What's nice about community service is that you can do it as a family. I encourage all families to work together to help make the world a better place. As the saying goes, "Charity begins at home." It's such a rich and rewarding experience and really opens up a child's eyes to what disadvantages, heartache, and hardships look like. Participation in charitable events also helps a child see that the world is bigger than he or she is, and that selfishness is not a desired trait. Participation in causes also gives definition to the importance of the work of charitable organizations. Further, it fosters accountability to the community.

## The Fourth Secret of Accountability: *Work*

My sisters and I had jobs in high school, as did many of our friends. It was just what you did if you wanted more spending money than your five- or ten-dollar weekly allowance—that is, if you *had* an allowance to begin with. Teenagers were expected to work for their own spending money.

Work was not something thrust upon us; we instinctively knew that hard work yielded great benefits. I even remember my mother having summer jobs like teaching summer school to earn extra income. However, one of my most vivid realizations of how difficult it must have been to raise us and to see us through college was the summer she also worked in the deli department at a local supermarket to make ends meet.

Seeing my mother in her uniform for the first time was a real shock. Mom, who was generally runway ready and the epitome of social grace, stood there in a soiled blue smock slicing meat, smiling proudly as I watched.

**Personnel** . . . Congratulations to Kathy Massie who was recently selected to be the new employment assistant in the Personnel Department. Previously, Mrs. Massie served as the secretary to the Department of Education and Training. Len Daugherty recently returned from vacationing back home in Arizona. Bernard Harris and Paul Slagenweit are also back from vacations. If Dorothy Watford's chest seems to be swelled these days, it's because her son, a Marine sergeant, is doing well as a professional boxer stationed at Camp Pendleton, California. We will miss Jo Anne Flowers, the Norfolk State student who worked in the Credit Union for the summer . . . **Dorothy Watford**

**Pathology** . . . Our congratulations to Felix Arintoc who has a new baby daughter "Elena Marie" and to Nellie Dabu who has a new baby daughter "Jayne." It's September wedding bells for Jeanette Byrum (Hematology) and Gayle Saperstein (Collecting Pool). A special "Hurrah" for Madeline Ducate who received her Master's Degree. Pathology extends a warm welcome to new employees Sue Quintero, Sandra Carpenter, Beverly Yarn, Tony Kelly and Gayle Saperstein. We say farewell and good luck to Wanda Pitt, Regina Overton and Karen Widener . . . **Marlene Miller**

**Security** . . . Wishes to welcome aboard our second lady Security Officer Nikki Potter. Good luck to departing Security Officer Lloyd White who will be sincerely missed. Lloyd is continuing his education at Old Dominion University for his degree . . . **Dan McMillian**

**Central Service** . . . Welcome to Miriam Burgess, RN, back from vacation and to George Sutton back from a medical leave. Thanks to Barbara Simiele for filling in for Ruth Rapp, secretary, while she was on vacation . . . **Deloris Allen**

**LIFE**
**IN GENERAL**

Published by and for the Employees of Norfolk General Hospital A Division of Medical Center Hospitals 600 Gresham Drive Norfolk, Virginia 23507

Robert L. Neal, Jr.     Administrator
Mahla E. Swinford       Editor
Isaiah N. Robinson      Photographer

*Double Exposure! That's what these girls would have had if they'd stayed out in the rain much longer for this picture. These two adorable twins, Eileen and Francine Olds, are members of the first graduating class of the Ward Secretaries' Training Course. The identical cars on which they are sitting are two new Dodge Darts recently purchased by Norfolk General to replace the station wagon which has been retired to the Service Center. To check out the cars for use on official hospital business, contact Diana Miles, Administration. To check out the twins, drop by Floors 7B and 8A on weekends.*

## personality profiles

# Twins Lead Double Life

Two of Chesapeake's most adorable identical twins Eileen and Francine Olds are ward secretaries at Norfolk General Hospital. These two look alikes came to NGH last spring after enrolling in the Industrial Cooperative Training Course at Indian River High School for students interested in medical careers. Eileen hopes one day to be a psychiatrist; but Francine, noting the additional years of higher education that psychiatry would take, says she would be happy becoming a psycho-therapist.

Both graduates of the first ward secretaries' training course, the girls worked full time all summer at Norfolk General "on call" basis — different stations, different shifts. Now that school is back in session, the twins have settled down to working weekend shifts on specific floors. Francine on 7B says she likes being out on her own; while Eileen, who feels right at home on 8A, enjoys knowing that the responsibility of doing a good job rests entirely with her.

These two look alikes have also made outstanding accomplishments on an individual basis. Eileen is president of the Senior Class at Indian River High School, while Francine serves as president of the National Honor Society. Both were delegates to the state's Model General Assembly, and both have served as junior varsity and varsity cheerleaders. Francine was the school's delegate to Girl's State, but she is quick to add that her sister was selected first alternate.

What are the twins planning after graduation? They hope to work at Norfolk General full time again next summer. Then, it's off to college — the University of North Carolina at Chapel Hill. "If we're accepted," Francine says, "we don't plan on rooming together, but we would like to be on the same floor."

"We've always enjoyed being twins — dressed alike, had the same friends, same interests. Some people say we are too close," Eileen added, "but we don't see it that way. We just feel really fortunate to have been born twins — it's great having someone around to encourage you all the time." For instance, when it comes time for one of them to run for office, they talk about it, decide who will run and who will help. When Eileen ran for president of the Senior Class, Francine served as her campaign manager.

What is the longest the twins have ever been apart? One month — which took place recently while they were abroad as part of an International Exchange Program between the Hinginbrook School in Huntington, England and Indian River High School. "We were gone one month. The first week we spent in London, but the remaining three weeks we lived with different English families — the highlight of our trip. We were quite surprised to find an English language barrier sometimes existed. The same words often had totally different meanings," Francine added.

*Norfolk General Hospital newsletter (1974)*

More than any words she might have said about that moment, watching her hold her head high and give her deli job the same enthusiasm and pride she gave her teaching job showed that she would do anything to support her children. Pride didn't get in her way when it came to her children's needs.

I never forgot that soiled smock in later years as I took jobs to help pay my way as a teenager and through college and law school. I can still remember the script from my first job as a telemarketer when I was sixteen years old: "We can offer you *Esquire, Argosy,* and *Mechanics Illustrated* magazines all at a low rate of …" Ugh, I hated that job, but not enough to want to stop working. I wanted a better job, but I knew that one would pay the bills, at least for a while.

My next job was a big deal and one that had roots in my high school. The Distributive Education Department at Indian River High in Chesapeake, Virginia, was looking for a few industrious students to apply for work as ward secretaries at an expanding medical complex. Fran and I were encouraged to apply on the recommendation of Mr. Ed Hughes, the director of the program. We were both accepted.

It was a real joy, not just to work with Fran but to also work at something that was more than menial labor and let me use my brain! Fran and I were busy most days transcribing doctors' orders, ordering medical supplies and pharmaceuticals, preparing patients' lab requests and medical test preps, as well as other clerical duties. It was a far cry from reciting a tired old script on the phone.

We loved it and were making grown folks' money! There is a picture of Fran and I sitting on the hoods of twin vehicles, which the hospital purchased, in our hospital uniforms that was disseminated in the hospital news publication. Boy, were we proud!

It is an experience I still value. I was forced to operate in an environment where there was no room for error, where I was forced to be mature *on a daily basis,* and where lifelong connections were made. Once you have a job like that, there's no going back to something like flipping burgers or telemarketing!

Working during high school or college breaks is a true shot in the arm for a child's sense of accountability. It opens up a new world of opportunity, a way to make new friends, earn one's own money, and solidify lifelong connections.

Like chores and other extracurricular activities, work teaches so many fundamental aspects of being accountable for actions and developing good skills outside of home and school, such as:

**Time management:** Often parents resist letting their kids get a part-time, after-school, or weekend job because it might interfere with their schoolwork. Certainly you should monitor your child's school and work performance to make sure it's a good fit. But I have observed in families where kids are allowed some part-time work that both areas of their lives improve dramatically. The act of juggling work, school, and extracurricular activities is perfected.

**Getting along with others:** In school, there are only two groups of people your child needs to worry about: other kids and teachers. In an after-school job, there are managers, supervisors, customers, and coworkers that may range from young children to the elderly. There are also different personality types, work ethics, and temperaments to navigate. Being employed is a great way to help your child grow into his or her own skin by working with others. One of the great gifts of personal accountability is birthed from being in direct contact with people from different walks in life and learning to be accountable to the correct people and principles.

## The Fifth Secret of Accountability: *Goals*

Help your child set and reach his or her goals. These can be goals like saving up for a new bike, taking the trash out twice a week, joining an extracurricular activity, reading one new book, or getting a better grade in chemistry next semester.

Frankly, with some children, when it comes to accountability, it's not the type of goal that counts the most but rather reaching the goal that helps them grow by leaps and bounds.

Many times, the end results of their efforts are not instantaneous. They go to school, but graduation is still a few years off. They take a test or turn in a report but won't know their grade until the end of the semester. But by setting short-term as well as long-term ones, kids get what they seek the most: instant gratification. Encourage goal setting and help them reap the benefit of feeling accomplished.

If trash days are Tuesday and Thursday, they can reach two goals a week, just like that. At the end of every Sunday, they know whether or not they've reached their goal of reading a book that week. Failure happens, but success can be addictive, and the more goals your child reaches, the more accustomed to success he or she will become.

## The Sixth Secret of Accountability: *Rules*

DOES YOUR HOUSE HAVE rules? I know your knee-jerk response will be, "Of course we do!" But check again. Does your child really have to be in bed, with lights out, by nine o'clock? Do you sometimes—or often—let him or her stay up until ten or even eleven?

Does he or she really have to finish the Brussels sprouts before leaving the table? Or do you just threaten him or her with that so that he or she will eat two more bites before you both finally give up and get tired of looking at each other over the tops of your water glasses? Children learn quickly what buttons to push, which rules are law, and which are, shall we say, a lot more flexible. The only way to hold kids accountable for their actions is to have rules and actually enforce them.

If you have a no-cussing policy in your house and your teenager uses vulgarities, how do you enforce it? Do you enforce it? How will he or she learn if there are no consequences for his or her actions?

## The Seventh Secret of Accountability: *Deadlines*

Life is full of open-ended questions and fluid assignments where both the starting line and the finish line keep moving. If a child isn't expected to finish something, reach a goal, or complete a task within a reasonable period, the incentive for doing so goes way down.

Giving children specific deadlines helps make them more accountable. Whether the goal is to complete a homework assignment, do a chore, sign up for an activity, or clean up after dinner, deadlines help keep kids on track. When kids are on track, they're likely to be more accountable as well.

## Parting Words about Accountability

There is such a fine line between dependence and independence for children, and it is a challenge for modern parents to oversee the balancing act. It is especially hard for those who want to cling to their children, protecting and shielding them from the harshness of the real world.

The truth is, the real world exists. They have to go out there someday, and the best way to prepare them for the challenges and expectations of teenage, young adult, and adult life is to allow them to take baby steps along the way, with you standing guard.

That same staggered approach is why schools add complexity and age-appropriate challenges with each advancing school year. That's also why valuable clubs such as the Girl Scouts, Boys and Girls Club, church groups, and YMCA exist: to support developmental challenges for children outside the home, build up their independence, and help them prepare for the future.

## Benchmarks of Accountability

- Accountability is at the heart of creating not just good kids, but good citizens. Our mother always taught us to be good citizens, and I believe we were better kids—and adults—for it.
- Teaching your child accountability helps him or her see his or her role in the family and in the world at large.
- Accountability counts, in large part, because it creates individuals who can grow and learn individually or, when necessary, as part of a group.

# Chapter 3

## The Power of **Purpose**

WHAT CAN WE GIVE our children if not purpose? Children who have purpose can better distinguish between right and wrong, good and evil, and instant gratification and future potential.

Many, many times my mother reminded us that we had purpose. She did not use the word *purpose*, but that's what she was talking about nonetheless. She told us many times that her constant prayer was that her twins would go far.

In between having my sister Joan and having Fran and I some twelve years later, my mom bore a son. His name was Barry. Barry only lived two days. There was a lot of grief surrounding his death. All I was told was that we had a brother who died while still in the hospital. As you can imagine, my mom was devastated by this loss. She told us about the hopelessness she felt, the ensuing depression, and how difficult it was to reconcile his death. In the midst of her grieving, she told of how she vividly recalls God speaking to her in consolation and how He said, "Don't worry; next time I will give you two!" And He did! With the fulfillment of this promise, Fran and I were born into *expectations*!

What she wanted more than anything for us was to be able to take care of ourselves, and, what's more, she wanted to live until we were grown to see that lifelong dream come to fruition. The mere telling of her expectations, in communicating the desires of her heart, gave us purpose. We knew that failure was not an option. Our purpose was to succeed in treating others fairly and being of service to others. Our purpose was to meet the twin expectations my mother had for us.

In short, kids with a sense of purpose know that there is more than just today, tomorrow, and the next day. There's a sincere and valid *reason for being here* and working toward a better today and tomorrow.

Conversely, children without a sense of purpose feel hopeless, restless, and even useless. Giving our young people a sense of purpose helps all of us in the long run.

## FINDING HOPE IN A HOPELESS AGE

Times are tough, and kids know it! They're not shielded from anything these days; not from the economy, political scandals, sex, drugs, violence, or the negative news on television. They are not protected from very adult matters that used to be beyond their scope of interest. It is no surprise now that education and other purposeful things take a backseat to much of the garbage now in their lives.

Educational programs, achievements, and personnel are not given sufficient attention. Every year our local paper publishes the salaries of its public school teachers, and they are abysmal. Can you imagine? It used to be that education and good teachers were priceless, regardless of what it said on my mother's pay stub once a month. Our job, as children, was simply to go to school. Adult things were for adults. Today, for most children, there is no mystery, no mystique, about adult life or the negative aspects of the future.

War, poverty, disease, the environment, and a million other depressing headlines are just part of our kids' daily routine. Without a filter, modern children can truly begin to believe that life is hopeless, the future is doomed, and the sky is really falling. (My mom read *Chicken Little* to us a thousand times.)

We are their filter. The media can be a hungry, sensational beast and runs 24/7, 365 days a year. The only reliable antidote to the message it screams all day long is us. We can explain, soften, or even poke holes in the specious reasoning used by most sensationalism our kids hear on a daily basis.

We can explain that not only are there two sides to every story, but that there are shades of gray. The fact is that these are grim times indeed. But there is so much about life to enjoy; share that with your kids and let them know that all is far from lost. Still, it is no wonder that it is difficult to make education and future aspirations a priority.

Good times, good people, good jobs, and good experiences await them, but they'll never know it if you're not there to be the antidote to the hopelessness that children can feel when assaulted by the realities of life too soon.

## EIGHT WAYS TO GIVE YOUR CHILD PURPOSE

Purpose is another antidote to hopelessness; it gives children a reason to believe not just in themselves but in their future. We focus too little on purpose these days. We celebrate the daily and even the hourly, but not the future. Kids need to know that the future exists, and that their future is bright.

In fact, children are a blank slate and the only ones whose lives haven't been sullied by scandal, mistakes, regrets, and missteps. They are at the starting line of a grand adventure, and they need to hear that *with purpose*, their lives can have meaning and a real impact on the world around them.

Your child doesn't necessarily need to know what his or her calling, or purpose, might be by the age of six! But purpose is more than that; it's about finding a reason to persevere through the bad times, and it's about having something to look forward to. It's about having hope!

Don't let your preconceived notions about what is or isn't important interfere with your child's sense of purpose. Today isn't like it used to be, even a few short years ago. We used spend hours in Ma Bruce's (our maternal grandmother's) house in the country, standing by the road and gesturing for the tractor trailer drivers to honk their horns at us. Much of our playtime was simplistic. I can't imagine parents of my generation encouraging us to major in Monopoly or truck sighting or jumping around on a pogo stick as a way of life, but today there are valid, lucrative, and meaningful careers in video games, extreme sports, computer technology, movies, music, writing, television, debating, journalism, graphic design, and a host of other subjects that kids can become very interested in even at an early age.

Folks like Tony Hawk and Shawn White have become viable and very visible brand names—spawning entire industries—thanks to their love for, support of, and interest in skating and snowboarding, respectively. So if two extreme sports enthusiasts can create entire industries *and* inspire kids to get outdoors and be more active with their passions, who's to say what your child's hobby might turn into?

*My Indian River High School cheering squad*

Even service jobs like mowing lawns and home repair can be extremely fruitful and purposeful jobs for kids who are handy and can go around the neighborhood on weekends and during the summer "practicing their purpose."

With kids, purposes come and go. They may take up golfing at a young age, switch to the saxophone, put that down for the drums, and then pick up a skateboard. Active minds breed active curiosities, and there is nothing more exciting than watching a child get excited about something new. Let them!

Encourage your child to try new things, multiple things, and return to old ones. Indulge his or her whims and curiosities within reason, secure in the knowledge that a child with passion is a child who is finding his or her purpose.

Here are nine simple ways to encourage your child to find his or her purpose at any age:

**The First Way to Give Children a Purpose:** *Listen to Them*

What are your child's hopes and fears? What are his or her worries, doubts, and anxieties? It's easy to look at a happy, smiling child and assume all is okay—that is, until you dig a little deeper.

It doesn't take much to get children talking. In fact, once the floodgates open, they can be hard to stop! When you take the time to ask a child a simple question, the response he or she gives and the appreciation he or she shows for actually being listened to can be genuinely surprising.

Kids need to know that their feelings are recognized and what they have to say about those feelings is valued. Listening is a simple task we often overlook because our lives are so busy and our kids seem happy. Look a little closer, talk a little longer, and listen a little better, and you can help your child craft his or her purpose gradually over time.

**The Second Way to Give Children a Purpose:** *Guide Them*

Guidance is so critical to helping an enthusiastic child make the right, informed choices about a passion or purpose. It can be something as simple as helping a growing boy pick out the right mouthpiece for his first football practice, helping him melt the form and fit it to his teeth. Or it can be as challenging as looking into creative writing programs for next summer. What seems to you to be no big deal may be huge for him. Guide your child so that he doesn't lose interest just because navigating the process seems daunting.

Your child may not play another season of football again, and that creative writing program may never pan out, but what will stand out is your enthusiasm, your presence, your participation, and, above all, your guidance

**The Third Way to Give Children a Purpose:** *Indulge Them*

It's okay for your child to have a hobby, a skill, a phase, a passing fancy, or even a fleeting whim; in fact, it's only natural. Then again, it may be necessary to put limits on your child's enthusiasm.

For instance, if your child is following a particular sports team or musical group, you could let him or her hang posters on his or her wall but not the living room wall! Allow your child to practice with his or her new band, but only until a reasonable hour.

Having a purpose or passion is no excuse for having the run of the house. That said, there's nothing wrong with a parent showing a little indulgence for his or her child's purpose or passion.

I once read how Steven Spielberg used to regularly enlist his parents' help in making his "little 16 millimeter" films growing up; they willingly indulged their young boy and no doubt would have kept indulging him even if he hadn't become one of the world's most famous filmmakers. For me, our front yard served as the practice field for cheerleading practice, and our garage was the laboratory for many creations, just as Aunt Ellen's front porch in Siler City, North Carolina, became the stage for the cousins' annual talent show.

Indulgence shouldn't be taken as a sign that the child has free reign of the household budget or the house, for that matter. But it should be taken as a sign that his or her parents fully support his or her interests and are eager to help him or her achieve his or her desired goals. And that kind of indulgence is good for everyone involved.

## The Fourth Way to Give Children a Purpose: *Join Them*

Before you completely disregard your son's love of skateboarding, for example, spend an afternoon at the local skate park. You may just find that not only is your child good, he's really good. Or even if he's not, maybe he's just really happy. And maybe the other kids there are happy too, and you find out that they're really good kids.

Before you discount your daughter's choice to go into cheerleading over an academic club, meet some of the other girls or even the coach. Perhaps you'll discover that one of the prerequisites for joining the cheerleading squad and staying on the team is a 3.0 GPA.

Yes, children go through phases as quickly as they tear through a dozen cookies and a gallon of milk, but each phase is a building block toward identifying their purpose. Extracurricular activities are actually "extra clarity" activities.

My mother used to joke that her car could drive itself to our school because of the number of times it went there each week for cheerleading practice, sporting events, student government meetings, honor society programs, and other activities.

I can only imagine how the demands of all our school projects encroached on her time, but as with most things, she did it without a hint that it was ever a bother. In later years, we talked about the toll it must have taken, and she let me know that she preferred doing it herself rather than regularly leaving us in the hands of other parents or carpools.

Whenever I am asked to summarize what parents can do to keep their children out of trouble, the short answer is threefold:

- Know where they are.
- Know who they are with.
- Whenever possible, go there with them.

## The Fifth Way to Give Children a Purpose: *Encourage Them*

What do you do to encourage your child's passion? Do you attend her school plays? Watch his football games? Go to her beauty pageants? Tag along to his sci-fi convention? Of course you do, but do you do it relentlessly and with enthusiasm? There is nothing worse than a whining parent.

Talk is cheap, but actions speak volumes, particularly when it comes to parenting purposeful children. You don't need to quit your job and follow your children's favorite band around the country, but when you can, show that you care by simply showing up.

That could mean something as simple as

- helping them build from their Lego kits;
- watching them play Super Mario or Wii Resort;
- reading part of their Goosebumps or Vampirates series;
- picking up some supplies for their movie monster diorama on the way home from work;
- inquiring about the newest game card in their collection;
- watching them try out a new cheer; or
- finding out what paintball really is.

It doesn't take much to show your children some encouragement when it comes to their purpose; sometimes, all it takes is literally showing up.

## The Sixth Way to Give Children a Purpose: *Support Them*

The world's children need support no matter what they're into, even if it's not a passion of yours. It's easier to take time off work to coach or watch your child's basketball team if you lettered in that sport in high school and even played for your college team. But what if your kid's into skateboarding, gaming, reading, or ballet? Will your child still have your support?

Support isn't necessarily financial. Just showing up at a game or two, a recital, or a weekend debate can send the message that you care, that you're there, and that you always will be. Sounds simple enough, but do it even when your child says it's okay that you don't.

Even if it was not expected, I always knew in the back of my mind that my mom would show up. In my adult life, she even liked to watch me preside over cases in my courtroom and also worked (more as a proud mama than anything else) in Fran's medical office. That support and confirmation meant the world.

Even if your job or other commitments don't afford you the luxury of being there in person, be there in spirit. Help your daughter with her talent show costume, or help your son design a new label for his skateboard. There are so many ways to support your child's passion that don't involve money, only your commitment to their purpose.

Some of the fondest memories I have are of my mom watching us just play. I can only imagine what she must have thought as she watched us play with our Strange Change Machine (an instrument that heated hard plastic squares that transformed into animal creatures after they reached a certain temperature) over and over.

I recall the enthusiasm as she joined in helping us transfer images from the funny paper onto Silly Putty. Thinking of her on the floor with us contorting her body to play Twister brings a smile to my face even now. Of course these toys are remnants of the past, as video games and console systems have replaced them, but there is still room for parents to get in on the action. I also vividly remember the excitement she shared when Santa Claus brought Fran her most coveted gift: a Nancy Nurse doll.

I swear, she played with that doll 24/7. Even then her passion for the healing profession was evident. That little seven-year-old grew up to become a nurse herself before going on to become a physician. Passion often develops early. Indulging that passion is critical.

## The Seventh Way to Give Children a Purpose: *Critique Them*

One way to turn a passion into a purpose is to help your child take it more seriously. Let's say your son picks up the guitar and starts strumming away; buy him some sheet music or even a lesson or two for his birthday or Christmas. Show him you're as serious about his passion as he is, and see what happens; see if it sticks.

If he does learn how to play, ask him to play you a song. If it's good, let him know what was good about it—be specific. If it was a little off key or you can tell he hasn't been practicing enough, gently remind him that practice makes perfect.

Never discourage or put down a passion, and particularly a performance, and if your child is serious about his passion and wants it to become a purpose, some gentle, constructive criticism can help guide him in the right direction.

**The Eighth Way to Give Children a Purpose:** *Question Them*

Now more than ever there seem to be as many purposes as there are children. In other words, we are getting way beyond football stands and chess club here! So if your child is becoming passionate about something that is new to you, don't just shrug and move on; find out what it's all about.

If his skateboard is covered with weird symbols and designs, pick one and ask about it; you might be surprised to learn that it's the logo of your child's favorite band, which could lead to a whole other discussion.

If your child is suddenly into making jewelry or buying trading cards, ask who or what his or her favorite is and why; the answer might surprise you.

When you have time together, use it to further your understanding of your child's passion. If you have no idea what *spelunking* is (exploring caves) or what a *philatelist* does (collects stamps), ask, participate, and appreciate.

Oftentimes all it takes is an interest in your child's purpose to give him or her enough fuel to pursue it fondly, aggressively, and passionately.

## PARTING WORDS ABOUT PURPOSE

The title for this chapter says it all: there really *is* power in purpose. I see it every day when kids who were on the wrong path find a sport, club, group, mentor, hobby, or job and really get into it. They frequently make a 180-degree turn from the wrong path onto the right one—they literally transform into kids with a passion for life.

Today's kids live in a more complex, complicated, open, transparent world than ever before. Give them something to hope for by instilling in them a genuine love for life and appreciation for their natural talents and abilities.

Indulge their phases, support their hobbies, listen to their stories, and guide them toward interests that can help them grow, live, love, and learn. It is never too late for a child to turn around and find that guiding passion that clicks for them and changes everything.

All children need is a little patience, guidance, and understanding as they search for the purpose in their lives. And in many cases, the search can become a purpose unto itself!

Life is so much better, richer, and rewarding when it's lived with a purpose, don't you agree?

Childhood is a time filled with fads and fancy. By nurturing our children to explore their passions (within reason), we help nurture their purpose in life.

Never look down on a child's passion or purpose—try to understand it instead.

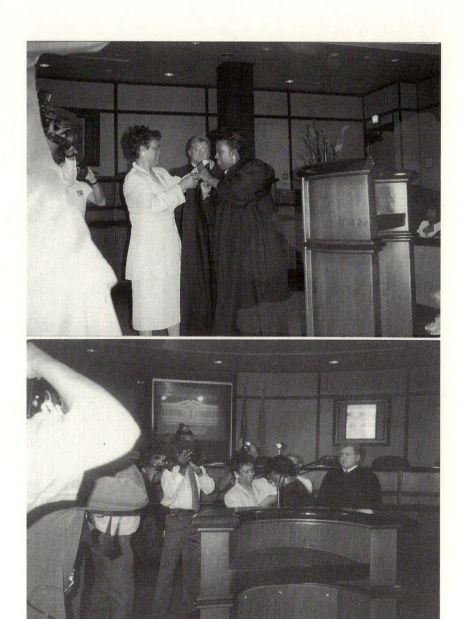

*My Mom Enrobing me at my Judicial Investiture*

*Chapter 4*

# There Is Freedom in **Discipline**

I RECENTLY HAD THE misfortune to be on the same flight with a boy named Herman and his mother—not the same row as Herman and his mother, not even the same aisle; just the same flight. I never got the mother's name; just Herman's. Here's why: the mother said it every five seconds.

"Herman, get your feet off that woman's chair."

"Herman, get that out of your mouth."

"Herman, where did you put Mommy's glasses?"

"Herman, stop messing with that man!"

Luckily it was a fairly short flight. Herman and his mother really got on my nerves! And I wasn't the only adult within earshot who wanted to give Herman a stern talking-to since his mother obviously wasn't going to do it. I know it's easy to be a backseat parent, but many on that plane knew exactly what little Herman needed: discipline.

So … why didn't his mother discipline him?

Despite the aggravation, it was hard not to feel bad for her. We only had to put up with Herman for the duration of the flight, but he was hardly six years old. She had many more years to go!

But as frustrated as that poor mother was, she was more hopeful than anything else—hopeful, I suppose, that she and Herman could get along and that she would not upset him; hopeful that letting him do whatever he pleased would make the situation better. What I saw in her face, however, was not the look of a parent rearing a child, but that of a friend looking for confirmation from another friend.

## Don't Be Their Friend, Be Their Parent

It's easy to think that being friends with our children is a great way to raise them, but in fact it's merely the easiest way. It lets us off the hook by indulging them too often simply to avoid a tantrum or their being mad at us for actually enforcing a rule or keeping them to their word.

Trying to be "cool people" with our kids merely confuses them. This isn't to say that you have to try to be something you're not, but many parents dumb down their behavior to try to become their child's peer or even their child's friend. They have friends at school, out on the street, in their clubs, and in sporting events. When they get home, they expect a parent, not a friend.

Kids don't need another friend; they need a parent. My mom knew this. She was firm when discipline was necessary, with good reason and with good results!

Even though we were keenly aware of our mother's youthful appearance, as well as her outrageous humor and ability to clown around with us frequently, just one look from her told us when foolishness would not be tolerated. What was right or wrong was not negotiable.

She said it; that settled it!

The key to discipline is being consistent, firm, and fair. Too many parents skip discipline because, frankly, it's harder to be hard on one's children than to be seen as the good guy, the friend, or the peer.

## There Is Freedom in Discipline

We often think our rules are too harsh or unnecessary for today's kids, but the fact is *rules are exactly what they need*. If the word *rules* still sounds too harsh, don't think of them that way; think of them as … guardrails.

What are guardrails but boundaries along life's path, barriers erected to keep us from driving our cars off the side of the road?

Some grown-ups need to master the discipline of dishing out discipline!

Seriously though, a child without discipline—without emotional, physical, and even spiritual guardrails—is like a sports car heading for Dead Man's Curve with both feet on the gas!

Frankly, children don't know any better; that's what we're here for. I should amend that: they don't know any better until they're taught to know better, and that's where we come in.

I once heard someone describe a child with no discipline as suffering from another form of child abuse. At the time, I thought that determination was a little severe. Now I'm not so sure. That person was saying that those parents who fail to discipline are endangering their children, placing them in harm's way, and forcing them to be ill-prepared for the adult world.

And that adult world, like it or not, is coming sooner and sooner for our children. Girls are dressing older, boys are dressing recklessly, and boys and girls are dating sooner. The Internet, especially social-networking sites, and cell phones have created "mini-adults" of children, who now think nothing of acting up, and out, in living color. The fact is, today's kids need more discipline, not less, because they are adultlike much, much sooner than ever before. Proper discipline should mean that *wherever children show out, parents show up!*

While it's much easier at times to let kids get away with not following the rules at home, what does that say to them about rules in the real world? That they're not important? That no one else follows them? That they're too good to follow them?

When I say that there is freedom in discipline, what I mean is that when guardrails are in place, kids know their boundaries. For instance:

- If a child knows his or her curfew is at eleven, he or she also knows that he or she is free to stay out until 10:59.
- If your child knows he or she needs to keep a B average to continue working his or her after-school job at the mall, he or she knows what's expected of him or her and is free to decide whether to keep the job.
- If your child knows he or she is not supposed to hang out at the skate park or the surf shop without a chaperone, he or she at least knows he or she is free to hang out at the park or the playground around the corner.

These rules, or guardrails, give kids the boundaries they need to discern good from bad, right from wrong, and hopefully everything in between.

I will never forget the time when I was in high school and came home from a date after Puddin's well-established curfew. The screen door was locked and the wooden door to the house was dead-bolted. Of course, this was all done purposefully so that I had to ring the doorbell and wake my mother up when I finally arrived home. I rang the bell, she answered, and the rest was history; that I still recall to this day. Let's just say it did not have a happy ending.

Quite honestly, some kids do *not* know what's expected of them. I'm presented every day with good kids who've gone bad simply because they didn't understand where to draw the line between good and bad or right and wrong.

Disciplining a child doesn't make you a bad guy; it makes you a parent.

## FIVE REASONS WHY KIDS NEED—AND SECRETLY WANT—DISCIPLINE

If you're still on the fence about discipline and its purpose or if your child keeps asking, "Why do I need all these rules?" here are five good reasons why:

### The First Reason Kids Need Discipline: *Respect*

Bottom line: Kids who don't have respect for you won't respect anybody else—least of all themselves. Parents earn respect and kids learn it when parents say no and mean it—when they draw a line in the sand and stick to it.

We often see parents out in public putting their sense of discipline on display. You can see it in the grocery store, where little Susan has a box of cereal in her hand that she's snatched off the shelf, even when her mother asked her very politely "not to do that."

"Put that back, Susan," Mom says.

"No," Susan replies. "I want it."

"But we already have a box of cereal in the basket, honey."

"I want *this* one!"

"But, Susan, you said you wanted the other one."

"Uh huh, I want this one now!"

"Okay, honey, if that's the one you want, we have to put this other one back."

*"No!"* replies Susan loudly as poor Mom looks around to see if anyone is noticing the scene. *"I want both of them!"*

"You can only have one, Susan. Now, which will it be?"

"Both!"

"One!"

"Both!"

"Susan, now, Mommy's trying to be fair. I'm happy to let you have one box of cereal, but not two. How many do we have in the cart now? Two, that's right, so ..."

But Susan is having none of it. She screams, cries, and carries on and finally her mom says, "Well, just this one time ..." And off they go, onto the next aisle where Susan will want two types of jam, juice, soda, or chips.

Again, I'm not trying to judge another parent's handling of her own child, although I'm tempted to at times, but we've all seen this same scenario go down too often to be amused any longer.

If my sisters or I had insisted on behaving like that, the mere threat issued by my mother to abandon her cart and take us home would have solved the problem—period, end of story. We were expected to behave both at home and in public, not because of what others might think, but because we were supposed to.

If Mom said one box of cereal, fine; we had a choice, and we chose. Sometimes we chose wrong, so the next time we'd choose right. It was a learning experience because it taught us to operate within the constraints of the rules.

Again, it's all about the guardrails. Discipline isn't saying you can't have any cereal (unless of course that's your rule!). It's about saying, "You can't have every type of cereal."

What it comes down to is respect—the kind of respect parents teach when they make rules and expect their children to follow them. But you're not just teaching them to respect you when you enforce the rules; you're teaching them to respect all people because rules help us all get along.

Rules help school go smoother, work go smoother, and subway rides go smoother. Rules are, in fact, a parent's responsibility because if you don't teach them at home, there won't be time—or teachers—later.

## The Second Reason Kids Need Discipline: *Consequences*

FOR MANY CHILDREN, THE trouble begins when their actions have no consequences, or when it at least feels that way to them, when they can always get away with snatching that second box of cereal on that shelf simply by crying, screaming, or throwing a tantrum.

When kids are constantly told that it's not their fault or when the blame is placed on the teacher, the principal, the counselor, the friend, or the enemy, there is no lesson being taught.

Kids without consequences are kids without guardrails, speeding toward destruction. I'm not exaggerating when I say that a childhood without consequences only yields adults who feel no responsibility for anyone or anything.

Why should they? If they just cry, blame, throw a fit, or look really tough, people will give them what they want. That's how they've grown up; that's how they will be when they are grown!

In reality, we live in a world where many, many people have grown up experiencing and, thus, expecting no consequences for their behavior. I am constantly amazed, as I'm sure you are as well, by the so-called adults we witness who continue to act like undisciplined children.

If you don't believe me, wait until the next time you need to deal with the public—say, at the DMV when your license is up for renewal—and you'll see what I mean. It's easy to say, as my mom did growing up, that some of these folks weren't "raised right," but in some ways many adults were never "raised" at all.

Now many of our children are growing up the same way, with no rules, discipline, or consequences. Again, I'm not trying to judge or even generalize, but if you're nodding your head right now, you know what I mean.

When kids have no discipline, they get no consequences for their behavior. And having no consequences gives them the wrong kind of freedom to act as they wish, whenever they wish:

- They can speak out of turn in class because even if the teacher reprimands them, no one at home will ever notice.
- They can act up in the cafeteria because even if they get detention, no one at home takes further action.
- They can get home late from school because nobody at home remembers if there are clubs they've joined or sports they might be playing.
- They can hang out at all times and places on the weekend because no one at home ever checks to see where they're going or who their friends might be.

You can see how this will affect classroom discipline, grades, social interaction, peer groups, and even a child's future as he or she spends less and less time in school and more and more time at home or on suspension.

So much of what happens around discipline is about parents preparing their children for success, not failure. I know it can be challenging to lay down the law and stick to it, but think of what you're doing to your children if you don't, and what you're doing *for* your child when you do!

### The Third Reason Kids Need Discipline: *Growth*

Kids grow when they learn, and, above all, rules help them learn. They learn

- the difference between right and wrong;
- empathy for other people;
- the limits of your patience; and
- the way things are done.

In the same way, you teach your child to swim and tie his or her shoe, and you teach him or her rules about life to keep him or her safe, happy, and productive as he or she grows into a young person and then a young adult.

There are so many immature children—kids who may look big for their age, or who appear tougher than most adults I encounter, but who have had little to no emotional development to enable them to act and engage as adults.

When a child is left to fend for himself or herself, he or she may get physically bigger, but this is hardly true growth. True growth happens when we learn, and kids learn by trial and error.

Unfortunately, with many of today's kids, it is all trial, no recognition of error, thus … no growth. They make mistake after mistake, break rule after rule, and … nothing.

Children learn when they do something right and are rewarded for it or, more often than not, when they do something wrong and are scolded, lectured, or even punished for it. These are not bad words because they are helping your child to grow.

A lack of discipline at home leads to a lack of appreciation for rules in society, in school, on the street, on the job, and in life. It also leads to a lack of growth, which can allow for children to become adults in chronological age but still not *grow*, if you know what I mean. In many ways, no matter how big they are, they are still children and will be for life.

### The Fourth Reason Kids Need Discipline: *Success*

For you and for your child, having rules and sticking to them is one of life's first lessons in *success*. If you can succeed at following rules, you can succeed at a host of other success habits, such as:

**Time management:** Having a curfew, knowing the trash has to be at the curb by seven in the morning, doing homework before dinner, turning in a book report on the day it's due—these lessons in discipline all help teach your child time management.

**Goal setting:** I can clearly remember my mother helping me set goals for particular achievements I wanted to make during school. Thanks to her help, it got to the point where I could form a timeline in my mind for what I'd need to do, by a particular date, in order to succeed. Whether it was writing my speech, leaving time to rehearse before I had to give the speech, or giving myself plenty of time to study for an upcoming exam, I could clearly set goals and reach them by a particular deadline. Naturally, that skill was transferable to my adult life.

**Following directions:** What are rules but directions for how to live? The more your child learns to keep a curfew, obey a direct order, wash the dishes, or pick one cereal, the more he or she will be able to follow directions in school, on the job, or as a fully functioning adult.

**Internal rewards:** My sisters and I felt good when we achieved something positive. A great test score, a winning game, a full piggy bank, or a special award were true achievements that deserved—and received—rewards. Sometimes they were external, like a trip to the ice-cream parlor or a new dress, but other times it was simply my mother's praise along with personal satisfaction. Later, the rewards were more internal: the happy feeling of contentment and the satisfaction of a job well done. It's my opinion that winning my mother's approval in my early years through following rules and learning discipline helped me take satisfaction in my own accomplishments in later years.

So much of what bothered my classmates about high school—getting to class on time, turning in homework properly formatted, being prepared for a pop quiz—hardly phased me and my sisters. We knew from Mom's discipline how to set and keep goals and how to apply ourselves to meet a deadline, even if it was only internal.

Frankly, I thank my mother every day for teaching me discipline at such a young age—not to say that I went through my formative years unruffled or without my share of mistakes, but the mistakes (and dramas) were much fewer because I worked to fulfill my own goals.

### The Fifth Reason Kids Need Discipline: *Other Kids!*

Discipline might not be as big of an issue if your child lived in a vacuum. Unfortunately, we must all let our kids roam free at some point, and that brings them into direct contact with … other kids!

Suddenly, your child has a new set of influencers—his or her peers. No longer are the adults in your child's life his or her only connection to the outside world.

So if we haven't done a good job of administering discipline before their school-age years, which these days can start as early as two or three years old when factoring in things like pre-K, we lose a significant amount of our influence the minute they start school.

It's more than just peer pressure; it's a whole new world, and many kids simply aren't prepared for the freedom that being out of the house up to eight or nine hours a day can bring.

Kids who have little to no discipline at home can often come up hard against a teacher's or a school's rules and find themselves looking to their new "friends" for support instead. If those friends also come from freewheeling homes, look out.

## Tips for Making Discipline a Priority

Talking about discipline is so much easier than actually doing it! But none of us would be very disciplined in our jobs if we merely talked about it, now would we?

While there are dozens of great books written about discipline, and each family will be unique when it comes to the rules in their home, I wouldn't feel like this chapter was complete if I didn't at least offer some tips about how to make discipline a priority in your home:

**Be reasonable:** No one is suggesting that your home resemble a maximum-security prison! Quite frankly, discipline is a personal thing (and I'm sorry if I've offended any parents by implying that you weren't doing your job!). Some homes are strict, some are lax, and yet children grow up with a firm sense of discipline. How? Well, as I've stated several times, discipline is transferable. Most kids who can remember the trash needs to be out before they go to school every Tuesday and Thursday can also keep a curfew and turn in their book reports on time.

**Be consistent:** My mom was never harsh with her discipline, but she was always firm. In fact, looking back, I think the reason my mother never really had to be harsh with us was because she was so firm. If we had encountered the grocery store scenario that I mentioned earlier, we would only have had to be yanked out of the grocery store once or twice before we would have realized, *Hey, she's really serious; we're going home!*

**Provide consequences:** Rules without consequences are like diets without restrictions—what's the point? You can't say, "Only one box of cereal per grocery store visit" and then come home with sixteen! That teaches kids absolutely nothing. I take that back: it teaches kids that rules without consequences are meaningless. This kind of give-and-take makes every new rule harder to enforce because your child knows you won't stick to it when push comes to shove. The more often consequences for bad behavior are reinforced—time out, no dessert, we're leaving the grocery store, etc.—the easier it will be the next time you try to enforce a new (or old) rule.

**Be realistic:** Everyone messes up from time to time, especially kids. I'm not advocating a house where everyone is perfect or that, for that matter, strives for perfection. What I am advocating is control—a house where your children are in control of their own actions because they have clear rules, discipline, and guidelines to help steady their maturation process. Giving in from time to time isn't against the law, nor should it be. Follow your instincts on vacation, over holidays, on weekends, whatever. If a child asks for permission to stay up past his or her bedtime, that's not so much breaking the rules as asking for permission to bend them. That's progress in my book!

**Compromise:** Kids will be kids. Childhood should be fun, and like I've said throughout this chapter, the rules are only there to provide guardrails for children to grow up comfortably in. Having realistic rules—like an eleven o'clock curfew instead of seven o'clock—shows your child that while you're not willing to let him or her roam free until three or four o'clock in the morning, you are willing to compromise.

**Lead by example:** Finally, try to avoid having one set of rules for your kids and another set of rules for you just because you're an adult. If your kids have to clear the table and wash their dishes, it would be helpful if you do too. Saying one thing and doing another is a quick way to undo all the discipline you're trying to instill. Instead, lead by example. Remember this truism: "I can show you better than I can tell you."

## Parting Words about Discipline

Disciplining a child can be hard. There's no doubt that it's hard for you and it's hard for your child. But who ever said parenting or childhood would be easy? There were many nights that my sister and I would debate the logic of a rule my mother was sticking to hard and fast. When she said no, she meant it. And we learned from it.

Why? Because she knew best. She had lived longer, learned more, and knew the difference between right and wrong. Ultimately, that's what discipline is: older, wiser people helping younger, more inexperienced people learn survival skills and the difference between right and wrong.

The fact is, kids don't know what's best for them because they haven't lived through the life lessons and don't have the hard-won instincts that we adults use every day.

I believe that only a caring, loving adult can effectively administer discipline because it is only when a proper relationship has been established that the rules can have meaning. When parents constantly yell at children, this makes it hard for children to differentiate when they are serious.

Along the same vein, I think my mom's discipline was as effective as it was because we knew she absolutely adored us and we absolutely adored her. It was a mutual respect combined with her consistently enforced discipline. Yelling and then laughing, not being consistent, fooling around and then suddenly getting serious, all of these mixed messages leave children feeling confused and, as a result, have little to no meaning for them.

Boil it down and the most common rules we teach our children are, for better or worse, about right and wrong and survival:

- "Look both ways before crossing the street."
- "Don't talk back to your teacher(s)."
- "I want you home before curfew!"
- "Treat others as you want to be treated!"
- "Put that back on the shelf; we haven't paid for it!"

Discipline may be hard, but the alternative is unfathomable. Adults must make the hard choices about raising children now that will help prepare them for the real world waiting right outside the door.

Don't we owe our children that much?

## BENCHMARKS OF DISCIPLINE

- There really is freedom in discipline; try it and see.
- Discipline isn't about turning bad kids good; it's about making good kids better.
- It's hard to enforce discipline in school when it's not reinforced out of school (i.e., at home).
- Don't consider yourself the bad guy for disciplining your child, but rather think of it as a favor that will prepare him or her for the future.

## Chapter 5

# Creating **Resilient** Children

PUDDIN' DIDN'T RAISE US to be quitters, not even a little. We *could* quit, of course. There wasn't a technical house rule against it; we just didn't, mainly because we knew it would disappoint Mom, but later on, it was because we knew we'd regret it and be just as disappointed as Mom.

If we entered a race, we stayed in it, even if we had no hope of winning. If we started something, we finished it, period. One of the great lessons these experiences taught us was to make better choices before starting something.

But, as children, we often went with our hearts instead of our heads, and we found ourselves in over our heads as a result. Even so, we stuck to our guns and stuck it out, and we always felt better for having done so.

## A FEW (CHOICE) WORDS ON RESILIENCE

One of the greatest gifts that my mother gave me and my sisters was the belief that we had the capacity to *rebound from anything*. The gift of resilience is a treasured blessing I carry from my youth, as I know my sisters do as well. It has seen us through many a trial and tribulation. The proper attitude about disappointment, obstacles, and even outright failure was conveyed early on by my mother. As she would say, "One monkey don't stop no show" or "This is just a fork in the road."

Of course, as a child, this response was not necessarily what I was looking for. At times it felt like a combination of tough love and being dismissed, as if my problems didn't matter enough to fret over.

However, the older I got, the more I realized that this was just further proof of my mother's determination to equip her children for survival in the real world. Helping us conquer those small defeats, which at the time seemed monumental, made the transition to greater challenges, defeats, and disappointments later in life more palatable.

Whether it was taking a test in school that seemed too hard, not making the cheerleading squad the first try, or breaking up with a boyfriend, our mother responded with a just-wait-and-see-what's-better-down-the-road attitude.

In the current cultural climate, children tend to want *everything* to go their way *now*. Worse still is the fact that oftentimes when that one thing does not go their way, it becomes the end of the road instead of that fork in the road that my mom warned us about.

"If at first you don't succeed, try, try again" may well be the first full sentence that my mother taught us! This gift of resilience that she gave to us was not one that she merely talked about, but that she practiced humbly herself.

For example, when my mother attempted to purchase a house as a newly divorced woman, the mortgage company initially denied the loan. The denial was not based on a lack of employment or credit status, but on her gender and marital status. The company also claimed that she needed the backing of her ex-husband.

Refusing to take no for an answer, my mother loaded us in the car and drove to the mortgage company headquarters in Richmond, Virginia, approximately one hundred miles from where we lived.

When she left her meeting with the company CEO, he had already decided that it was impossible to turn her down. She got that loan, and the house that she purchased was where we grew up and where my mom resided for more than forty-five years!

That house became the "command headquarters" for many lessons about resilience and perseverance over the years. That house, which she quickly turned into a home, was the foundation—both symbolically and realistically—of what can happen when children and families are encouraged to turn obstacles into stepping stones.

There are many times that I am still empowered and awestruck by my mother's tenacity. There are many times that I remember her call for resilience. Instead of instilling hate for the wrongdoer, or viewing the wrongdoing or setback as a signal to give up, my mother made it clear that our responsibility was to learn from the experience and then move on.

For instance, a few years after our move to our new home, it was our mother who again refused to accept the notion that her children would be excluded from attending a newly constructed elementary school just yards from our neighborhood.

After lobbying the school superintendent, we learned the day before the school year was to begin that he had acquiesced and was allowing us to attend. In doing so, my twin sister and I became the first to racially integrate the newest state-of-the-art elementary school in the city.

The next year when I was elected president of the student body in junior high school, Fran and I were still two of only a handful of African Americans in the school. I was so proud to have been given the honor, and I spent the summer before the school year that I was to serve preparing to assume my role. I even attended a Student Government Association (SGA) camp at Longwood College in Farmville, Virginia, designed to give us blueprints for SGA leadership.

However, shortly after returning from the camp, my school principal contacted us to advise that during the year of my presidency there would be no Student Government Association. What a letdown! Even in my thirteen-year-old mind, it seemed preposterous that all of a sudden the student government was abolished.

For the first time.

Ever.

My mother had to explain that everything in life is not fair, but that the disappointment would set the stage for future successes. And, once again, my mother was right! I went on to become president of my high school senior class, president of the Black Law Students Association at the Marshall-Wythe School of Law at the College of William and Mary, president of the local branch of the NAACP, and most recently president of the American Judges Association, the largest independent association of judges in the United States and Canada.

The same lesson was taught when Fran became the school spelling bee champion. Rather than congratulate her, the principal bolted over to shake the hand of the runner-up. Poor Fran was devastated. It took Puddin' to explain that nothing could take away from her brilliant win! "Mr. Austin, just didn't know how to shake a little black girl's hand."

Resilience—it's one of the greatest, longest-lasting gifts my mother ever gave me.

The above examples are all life lessons, teachable moments that my mother took advantage of. Every child deserves to be taught these survival skills. Suicide rates among teens have skyrocketed over the past decade. Recidivism among juvenile delinquents has grown exponentially. Why? In part it's because children with no hope for the future have become the norm in many communities. Much of this hopelessness and despair is prevalent because the art of resilience is not being taught or demonstrated.

There are many things that we can show children better than we can tell them. Resilience is one of them.

Instead of crying on their shoulders or "parent-ifying" children by dumping the weight of adult burdens on them, tell your children—and show them—as my mother did, what resilience and perseverance look like. Instill in them the acceptance that failure and disappointments are inevitable, but so is success when they are equipped with the gift of resilience.

Today, unfortunately, we see kids quitting—on projects, goals, programs, sports, and even themselves—quite often. Quitting isn't necessarily bad when done rarely and with good reason, but it can become a habit, even a lifestyle, if we quit too quickly or too often.

*Taking my oath as president of the American Judges Association with Brett and Bria (2007)*

The more often we quit, the less *durable* or *resilient* we become. That's why it's important that we recognize, and hopefully avoid, what I call the Seven Dangers of Quitting.

**The First Danger of Quitting:** *Quitting Increases Doubt*

When we quit something, we often wonder why we ever started it in the first place. Then we begin to wonder others things as well, like, *What's wrong with me? Will I ever succeed at something? Why do I quit so often? Why do I start so many things and never finish them?* Each question makes us doubt ourselves all the more.

Children have enough doubt in their lives. Help them battle doubt and inspire self-confidence by sticking to things, even if it makes life harder for a little while.

**The Second Danger of Quitting:** *Quitting Gives Us a Reputation*

Earlier I talked about labels and how positive ones can help kids later in life and negative ones can hurt them now *and* later. Right or wrong, the more often we quit the things we start, the less reliable we seem to others. Those with a reputation for quitting are not expected to finish or succeed. Don't let your child be among those labeled as quitters.

This trend can be seen on many modern résumés and job applications, where young applicants take multiple pages to list any and all the jobs they've had in the last few years. Some of them even wear their "leapfrogging" like a badge of courage. They never consider how it looks to future employers—like they've never stayed on a single job longer than two or three months.

**The Third Danger of Quitting:** *Quitting Is Addictive*

Like many bad habits, quitting is addictive. When we quit, and quit often, we create a legacy in which it's okay to quit something without considering the fallout or who else may get hurt in the process. It's easy to joke about a certain celebrity who was married seven times, quitting on each of them and leaving a trail of husbands behind. It often raised eyebrows because of the implied carelessness or lack of commitment. But the same can be inferred when you leave your boss, your team, your project, or your coworkers in a lurch when you simply fail to show up for work one Monday morning, or when you don't show up for practice or keep appointments time and time again. Starting and then quitting, quitting and starting can become a vicious cycle.

We know that teenagers change best friends weekly. However, pay close attention to discern between normal teenage behavior and a pattern of quitting, signs of disloyalty, or a lack of concern for others' feelings.

Even at fourteen years old, it is not okay to covet your close friend's girlfriend or boyfriend or kick that friend to the curb to get your own way. The same philosophy goes for giving children the authority and power to call the shots on the kind of relationship they have with an adult, especially a noncustodial parent. Again, reasonableness is key; children should not be allowed to quit relationships on a whim. When we teach our kids that it's okay to quit easily and often, we set them up for a life with no strong attachments, no fortitude, and no resilience.

### The Fourth Danger of Quitting: *Quitting Saps Our Strength*

The more often we quit, the less often we succeed. The less we succeed, the weaker we become. Facing challenges makes us stronger, not weaker.

There is something about facing a crisis—be it personal, professional, spiritual, or financial—that adds another layer of strength to our characters. Children need to solve problems, overcome obstacles, and succeed over challenges in order to feel strong. And the more they stick with something and see it through, the stronger and more resilient they will feel. There are times when the grass looks greener on the other side, but you still have to mow it sometimes! There is quiet strength in sticking to duties, commitments, and responsibilities. Life is full of assignments and they are not always pleasant. I think of my mother in that deli department trying to support her children and how she must have thought of quitting that job. But she had responsibilities and she needed to fill in the gap, so she did what she had to do. She was no quitter! I felt the same when I held down that telemarketing job. I couldn't wait to quit, but had to hold on until something better came along. Sticking to it made me stronger and made me appreciate my new job all the more.

### The Fifth Danger of Quitting: *Quitters Attract Quitters*

It's often said that we can tell what kind of people we are, and even the future we dictate, by the company we keep. I've often found in my own life that when I surround myself with people who are less motivated than I am, I tend to become less motivated as a result.

That is exactly the reason that my mom flatly prohibited us from associating more than coincidentally with others whom she felt would impart a "negative influence" on our lives. I now get how absolutely necessary it is for adult caretakers to screen the "friends" with whom their children associate.

The screening of friends by parents is crucial. It is mind-boggling that parents no longer bother to find out how or where their children met their friends, where their children's friends live, or who their parents are, and, eerily, they may never even meet the parents. Peers are so important and influential to children. It's critical that they are surrounded with positive influences rather than negative ones. It is impossible to assess the potential dangers of association if there is no interaction or meaningful knowledge about the contacts being made.

**The Sixth Danger of Quitting:** *Quitting Is Usually Done in Isolation*

I clearly remember exactly where I was when I strongly considered quitting law school. I had been up all night studying for a United Commercial Code (UCC) exam, and it just wasn't sinking in. In that instant, I had convinced myself that I was not cut out for law school even though I had done well and was about to finish my first semester of my second year.

Before making it official, all I needed was to have Fran agree with my assessment that law school was not for me. At the time, she was in her second year as a nurse at Duke University Hospital's Gynecology Oncology Unit. She too recalls the spot where she was standing when I made the frantic but resolute telephone call to her.

"No way!" she said emphatically. "Eileen, you're just tired; keep going. You'll see it'll all look better in the morning!" Thank God I reached her and that she had a clearer head at the time than I. I did not quit, and boy am I glad that I didn't!

The fact that I reached out to my twin sister helped me break the isolation I felt and saved me from quitting something I truly cared about. There is another lesson here as well: sometimes it takes caring intervention to derail quitting.

**The Seventh Danger of Quitting:** *Quitting Can Cause a Chain Reaction*

THE MORE YOU QUIT, the easier it is to quit. For example, quitting a few part-time jobs as a youth can lead to a habit of quitting bigger, more important, even dream jobs in adulthood. So many character traits are established in childhood. Sadly, quitting is no different. As responsible adults, we cannot allow our children to quit just because they want to. If all they know to do when life gets rough is quit, nothing will ever be permanent. When quitting becomes a habit, it's simple to walk out on a lease, never go back to a job, or run away from family and spousal responsibilities without looking back.

This tendency to quit one thing can lead to quitting two things, then two more, until our children are responsible for nobody and nothing—not even themselves.

*Law school graduation*

*Fran's medical school graduation*

## THE NEW SPIRIT OF RESILIENCE

NOT QUITTING HELPS US become the opposite: resilient! *Resilience* is a word we don't use often enough, but one that's particularly in need of a resurgence if we are to overcome the ever-increasing challenges that face our children.

Many of us grew up in awe of the Hollywood version of life—that if you simply want it bad enough, you can truly achieve anything in this country. But as adults, we learned soon enough that this isn't really the way the real world works. Hard work and persistence go a lot further than just wanting something.

Hard times and harder realities have taught us that lucking out is not the safest bet and that the "fame and fortune at any cost" mentality of our younger generations is at war with what we know to be the truth: *life isn't always fair.*

Creating children who can face adversity, disappointment, and even failure with a positive outlook and hope is one of the greatest gifts we can give them. This gift is called *resilience*!

## WHY RESILIENCE MATTERS

Resilience is critical because pain and adversity are unavoidable. In fact, life is fraught with pain: pain of rejection, pain of failure, pain of disappointment, pain of bullying, pain of overeating, pain of not eating enough, pain of grieving, and pain of losing. The only way to get past the pain to the sheer joy that awaits your child is to teach perseverance—how to stick with it and get through it—and that requires resilience.

According to TeenDepression.org, "Suicide is the third leading cause of death among adolescents and teenagers." We know that young people who commit suicide, or even attempt suicide, are filled with feelings of hopelessness, depression, and despair. This is the ultimate form that quitting can take because, in effect, these kids are quitting on life.

We can help our children avoid such feelings by giving them hope through problem-solving skills associated with sticking to something, overcoming an obstacle, or facing a challenge. Helping them go through and not just go around an obstacle is critical.

A child's sense of self can be rocky at best and fraught with insecurity and a decided lack of confidence. When we help our children to persevere and get through the hard times by doing the work that's required, we help build their confidence and problem-solving skills.

The path to a child's success starts early, and few things make that path clearer or straighter than resilience. To help your child become more resilient, remember to:

**Support strength:** If necessary, *help* your child be strong. If it means making changes on your part or even inconveniencing yourself for a little while, so be it. I believe strongly that, as far as sacrifices go, it's either pay now or pay later. Maybe your child has taken on a newspaper route that he or she is ready to quit after three tough days. Rather than let him or her quit and give up altogether, try to help him or her—at least for a little while—to stick with it until he or she can gradually do the newspaper route on his or her own, sans help. Like many things in life, sometimes our kids just need encouragement to stay with things rather than give up on them. Resist the temptation to give in to the whining and let your child take the easy way out at every turn. Encourage hardiness, strength, persistence, and resilience instead.

**Choose challenges:** I'm not encouraging you to go out of your way to make your child's life harder, but I *am* suggesting that you avoid making your child's life so easy that there are no challenges *at all*. Every now and then, set up a roadblock in a safe, controlled environment, get your child's input on resolution of the conflict, and then walk him or her through the reasoning necessary to tackle the issues involved. Encourage your children to be joiners, to take risks, and to be active, especially when it means trying new things.

**Discuss the options:** Children often act with a one-track, fast-track mentality. Because they may only know of one obvious way to resolve a problem or weather a storm, it is up to us to offer options. It is our duty to offer balance and well-reasoned solutions. Remember, children can't do better until they know better. As adults, we should have a much better perspective on the short- and long-term effects of giving up, caving in, and quitting.

**Stand firm:** If you and your child discuss the options, weigh the pros and cons, and agree beforehand on a plan of action and then if he or she wants to jump ship after only one day in the club, on the playing field, in the summer camp, behind the counter, or on the job, do your best to stand firm. Even when the waterworks and excuses start, it's critical that you stand firm so that your child can learn from your example. Fran and I both wanted so badly to quit piano lessons after the first few, but my mom was having none of it, especially after she had purchased a piano. I think much of the initial intrigue with playing was because of the genius talent we saw in our cousin Nedra. Her tiny hands made playing the piano appear so doable, and there were others on my father's side of the family tree who were also musically inclined. We jumped in, but the talent just wasn't there for us. Still, it was a commitment made, and the promises had to be kept, period. So while there are but a few songs I learned to play with proficiency, I am grateful for the fact that I have lots of music appreciation and just a little of skill, all because I was made to plow through a series of lessons.

**Protect them when you can, prepare them when you should:** Finally, because you're the parent; it's your responsibility to know when to prepare your child and when to protect him or her. If your child is truly unhappy in a situation and staying with it is going to do more harm than good, maybe quitting is the best option. Don't turn a blind eye or deaf ear to genuine signs that something may be wrong or truly not a fit. On the other hand, if it seems like the end of the world to your child but you think/feel/know better that after a day or two he or she will be all right, you should encourage, even insist, that your child keeps going. Remember, becoming more resilient really *is* for your child's own good!

## PARTING WORDS ABOUT RESILIENCE

Like so many of the gifts, habits, and tools in this book, resilience is learned. Growing up, quitting generally was not a viable option; we were led to adapt, gather resources, find a way, and do our best to make things work.

As guardians, it's only natural to want to protect our children from the harsh world outside. It requires vigilance to help them navigate the roadblocks that are bound to appear. But they have to be on their own someday. We do more for them by gradually preparing them to rebound than letting them succumb to the obstacles they encounter.

As I stated in the last section, it's our job to protect them when we can and prepare them when we should. However, oftentimes, we slip too easily into protection mode rather than preparation mode. This can lead to overprotection, which results in our children being underprepared. And we certainly don't want that.

## BENCHMARKS OF RESILIENCE

- Children need life lessons that they see demonstrated by adults, not just spoken.
- Children need adults as their advocates, enabling them to learn how the gift of resilience looks in action.
- Children benefit from viewing obstacles as works in progress with eventual positive outcomes.
- Children need to know that life will encompass disappointments, pitfalls, and distractions, but giving up is not the first line of defense.

# Chapter 6

## *Manners* Matter

I WAS DRIVING SOMEWHERE the other day and saw one of those professionally printed, stick-in-the-ground signs on the side of the road advertising a class on teen etiquette. I must admit that I was thoroughly tempted to call the number and shout into the receiver, "Yaaaay!" But I restrained myself.

It reminded me of what a friend told me a few years back when she shared with me an etiquette video and spoke of classes that she began offering under the title "Etiquette Divas." She felt that the refined process of learning social graces was not occurring enough. She felt that the era where children were appropriately taught manners needed a revival.

At that instant, that sign made me think that maybe my friend and I are not the only persons on the planet who think that *etiquette, manners,* and *civility* should be mandatory subject matter for all children, and also that more time should especially be devoted to teaching preteens and teenagers, one of today's most difficult audiences, about one of the world's greatest challenges: *being more polite.*

I did some investigating and discovered that there are dozens of courses for childhood etiquette popping up all over the country. From web classes to books to CDs to hands-on training to etiquette training for etiquette *trainers,* civility is making a comeback.

I feel that the need for a resurgence is so great partly because there has been a huge division in beliefs as to exactly who is responsible for teaching children manners and civility these days. Teachers? Parents? Society? I believe it should be part of the "home training" my mother often spoke about, and we as responsible caretakers should emphasize it early and often.

For me, it all comes back to an old standby—*personal accountability*. It's not so much a question of where or when for most people, but who. Apparently, many parents think schools should teach etiquette; schools seem to think it's only common sense that parents teach good manners and other related lessons. Therein lies the disconnect.

Unfortunately, it is the children who lose in this tug of war. If parents are expecting the schools to teach their kids civility, and teachers are expecting parents to do the same, and neither actually *are*, kids simply aren't learning the nuances anywhere. And when proper consideration for others, respectability, and manners are taught in one setting but not reinforced or required in the other, civility loses its relevance. When civility happens on occasion instead of habitually, that's worse than not teaching it at all. As a society we are becoming ruder by the second; our kids aren't being shielded from that trend. That rudeness is compounded when we fail to properly instruct children.

Manners matter now more than ever!

## WHY MANNERS MATTER

When I was growing up, we were taught that manners mattered simply because *other people mattered*. Manners were a way of verbally and physically communicating respect to another human being. Using good manners toward adults was confirmation that we respected their authority and seniority over us.

A kind word, a "Yes, sir" or "No, thank you," was all it took to say, "I respect you. I care about you." It was a lesson we learned early and learned well.

I guarantee you that *please* and *thank you* were among the first words my mother taught us; *pretty please* and *thank you very much* were even better. My mother was not rude, and she definitely would not tolerate rudeness from us.

Being polite and being civil are more than mere acts of respect; they are acts of basic human kindness.

We were taught to be polite to everyone, especially to grown folks. Today some children wear their surliness, disrespect, ill manners, and crudity as badges of honor. Unless it stops, I fear that we are raising an entire generation of heathens who will be woefully unprepared or underprepared for the basic rituals of modern life, to say nothing of living with empathy, compassion, and human decency.

Here are a few more reasons why manners must matter to you, your child, and the rest of the world as well:

**We don't live in a vacuum:** We need other people to survive. We depend on mail carriers, customer-service operators, policemen, and firemen. We routinely interact with colleagues, bosses, teachers, neighbors, and friends. When we are rude, disrespectful, or ill-mannered, we lose the respect of others and, hence, a host of opportunities to make friends, forge relationships, make advancements, or even make a living.

**Life does not end with graduation from formal education:** Life within the confines of school may seem like a world unto itself, but the world does not end when your child turns his or her tassel from one side to the other. Whether it is family-related, work-related, social, or professional, all types of relationships are dependent on the intricacies of human interaction. A lack of civility erects a wall of rudeness and signals a deficit in interpersonal relations between your child and society.

**Competition is everywhere:** It is getting harder and harder to gain entry into certain secondary schools, special programs, and colleges, and more competitive to get a good job and get ahead in an increasingly complex and success-driven world. An applicant who shows up for a coveted position on time, nicely dressed, with an accurate and professional résumé, and who can appropriately and intelligently interact during an interview without fumbling over social niceties has a distinct advantage over another applicant who lacks civility. Even the A student must meet certain social barometers to be considered for most positions, while kindness and courtesy will place a marginal candidate over the top! But more than in employment settings or on academic campuses, manners are a way of life. For a moment, think of it this way: teaching good manners is integral to raising good *kids*. That's ultimately what we want, isn't it?

**People do judge:** Major decisions and judgment calls are constantly being made based on first impressions. People judge us based on how we act, how we look, and what we say. If we want our kids to get an even shake at the best of life's opportunities, we have to share with them the cold hard facts of how outward appearances do count.

As much as we'd like to think that profiling and stereotyping are things of the past, unnecessary and sometimes-tragic incidents remind us that this is not the case.

It's more than just an ethnic or cultural thing. Today's generation gap is larger than ever because the culture of childhood has changed so rapidly. Today some kids go out of their way to be hard, have street creditability, and avoid looking weak such that it has alienated and intimidated a large portion of the adult population. Right or wrong, many adults are afraid of kids, particularly large groups of kids, and that's a shame.

There are enough unfair, ignorant judgments made against our children without the need to offer other reasons for them to be mislabeled and misunderstood. Having good manners can bridge the divide between children and those who would mischaracterize them simply because of how they look, act, behave, or "come off." Talking trash, cursing, using foul language, or disrespecting random strangers on the street isn't just disrespectful. These days it can be downright dangerous.

Manners can diffuse a lot of situations that might go badly, not just on the street but when applying for a job, getting into a college, or playing on a team as well. Manners mean opportunity, and that's one more reason why they matter so much.

Giving *proper guidance, mutual respect,* and *consistent reinforcement* can help our children to have good manners as well as good instincts for living a good life.

## MANNERS MATTER: *EIGHT (SIMPLE) STEPS TO A MORE CIVIL CHILD*

We have to get to a place where teaching our children manners is as common, routine, and dependable as teaching them to tie their shoelaces or brush their teeth. Manners are no less a survival skill than personal hygiene or safety.

So, to help you raise a more civil, mannered, and polite child, here are eight simple steps:

**Practice what you preach:** More than almost any other way, children learn by watching. If you are rude to telemarketers, random strangers who knock on the door, or even to each other, your child will pick up on this and do the same, perhaps even unconsciously. Threatening to curse somebody out or exhibiting road rage regularly gives children tacit permission to do the same. So if you want a more civil child, be a more civil adult. It sounds easy, but pay closer attention to your own attitude in and out of the home, and you might be surprised by how uncivil you sometimes behave. If you want your child to have good table manners, eat at the table! If you want your child to value other people's time, then stop showing up at Chuck E. Cheese's as everyone else is about to leave the birthday party! So before taking your child to task over his or her manners, stop and think about your own. Children learn so much at home, and manners—or the lack of good manners—say a lot about what goes on in your home.

**Seek outside help:** If manners and proper etiquette are important to you, or a sore spot with you and your child, seek help from others without having to reinvent the wheel. Buy a book or a course on DVD, or even hire a consultant or coach to train you and your family in proper etiquette. If your child works best in a peer-to-peer setting, enroll him or her in a special class like karate or judo. It may be worth the cost of admission to raise a civil child in an admittedly sometimes-uncivil world. Remember: pay now or pay later.

**Create a civil environment:** If your home is civil, it stands to reason your child will be as well. Are you polite to each other? Are you polite to your child? Are you polite to strangers? Do you eat dinner at the kitchen table, at least some nights? Do you use real plates and silverware or paper plates and plastic "sporks"? None of these behaviors are right or wrong, but if you really want to make manners a priority in your child's life, then the first and best place to start is in your own home.

We can't expect children to sit down in a restaurant and use the correct utensils if at home they are always standing over a counter eating chicken fingers and fries with their hands or watching TV while they down a pizza. And it's perfectly okay to consciously practice. I recall many times with my nephew and niece, Brett and Bria, going over various scenarios that related to proper dialogue, manners, and etiquette. "What if you were having dinner with President Obama? What would you do then?" I might ask, or, "What if you were seated next to your teacher at the movie theater?" or even, "What if you were introducing me to so-and-so?" Sometimes these play-acting scenarios help children learn a better, more polite reality.

**Include their friends:** Children like other children. They spend time with other children. Frankly, they tend to prefer the company of other children. Other children have power in their lives, so if you want to make your child more civil, more mannered, and more polite, it might serve you well to include your child's friends in your civility campaign. Invite them to a dinner where you teach, say, one piece of etiquette at a time. For instance, teach what is the proper way to introduce a friend to another friend, or which is the salad fork and which is the soup spoon, or how you set a table. Your child has play dates, right? Why not etiquette dates as well? It may seem far-fetched or even unpleasant at first, but it doesn't have to be. Serve good food! That's one way to get your child and his or her friends to buy in!

**Set boundaries:** Kids need boundaries. They need to know they can go this far and no further. If your rule is don't put your feet on the couch, stick with it. If you require that they not interrupt each other in the course of conversation and they do, you can't ignore it! If you think a word that they use is disrespectful, don't allow it in your home (without consequences). If one child's music is too loud while another child is trying to study, put a stop to it! Observing good manners goes beyond figuring out which dinner fork is which; it is also about observing boundaries. And, by the way, if you think they're having too much television screen time, limit it.

If the social-media obsession is getting out of hand, allow only so many hours on Facebook, Twitter, YouTube, or whatever! And if you are not familiar with these sites yourself, now is the time to check them out. If you think your child is texting too much, cut down on the hours or minutes he or she has for phone usage each month. If you want the family to eat at the table each night, only serve meals to those who show up, sit down, and plan to eat at the table. Playing by the rules is a major component of civility. Setting boundaries may be hard at first, but they're absolutely necessary, especially when you're teaching good manners.

**Take a class together:** I actually purchased my friend the etiquette diva's DVD, so I now know which lessons are included. Frankly, I was reminded of some fine points that I haven't been called on to practice often. Over the strong objections of then thirteen- and fifteen-year-old Bria and Brett, the DVD became the focus of a family movie night. Though not the most exciting thriller we've ever sat down to watch together, I think there was relief in just knowing that now they know what to do and have heard it from the perspective of an adult whom they don't personally know. I'm also tempted to require that they view it from time to time as a refresher for them. I doubt that I can convince them to download etiquette tips as an application on their smart phones, or make it a personal priority, but every little bit counts. And I know that taking an interest in and devoting time to them as they were instructed is an added bonus!

**All hands on deck:** If you have a big family, it can't just be one or two of you trying to have good manners; everybody needs to be on board. It's the same with a small family. The work you do with your child will quickly erode if the minute he or she walks away from the table, he or she sees everyone else busy eating with their hands off of the coffee table in front of the TV. Consistency is the key to civility, and that means everyone must be on message, together, with a concerted effort to have better manners as a family.

**Take a test run:** Finally, give your child's good manners a test drive by taking it out on the town! Go to a nice restaurant (it doesn't have to be expensive; just sit down with real silverware) and practice what you've been teaching at home, not just which one is the salad fork but how to be polite and interact socially with others. Work on "please" and "thank you," "yes, sir" and "no, ma'am" as the waitstaff serves. Work on being on time, being courteous, and, most importantly, enjoying the time as a polite family. Excursions like this one can be purposeful and powerful when done in the spirit of fellowship. Kids need us; they really do. What's more, they want us to be actively and purposefully involved in their lives. They may not say it—may not even show it—but it's true. The fact is, the time you take to help your child be better mannered and test drive those manners out in public may wind up being his or her fondest memories. Mark my words! I know that nothing meant more to me and my sisters than making my mother proud and seeing that pride reflected in her smiling face. Those are the memories I cherish still, and ones your child is sure to keep as well.

## Parting Words about Manners

Few children want to be rude just for the sake of it; most simply don't know better. If your child never hears, "Don't text at the table, dear; it's rude," he or she will simply assume it's not rude and continue to do so—be it at your house, a friend's house, a girlfriend's house, or on a job interview. I honestly know of a skilled office manager who was fired for texting someone while her boss was talking to her. Fired. Period. End of story.

I believe kids want to be good, even if it's inconvenient. That includes having good manners. They simply need guidance on how to act on their instincts and sometimes even against their instincts. Of course, that's where we come in!

## BENCHMARKS OF MANNERS

- Manners are not a lost art, just a neglected one.
- When manners matter to you and your child, it makes others feel like they also matter.
- Good manners are equally important inside and outside the home.
- Never is leading by example more important than when it comes to manners.

*Chapter 7*

# More **Independence** Sooner

WHEREVER YOU CAN AND whenever you can, encourage your children to be independent more often. While it may seem more nurturing to keep your child close to protect, isolate, and even insulate him or her from life's ills, the fact is that you're only delaying the inevitable and making it harder for him or her when he or she has to grow up, move out, and face reality.

The world is harsher than ever in its treatment of children. What the world does to our children—the way so many have had to know so much, so soon, just to get by—truly breaks my heart. Be it bullying, peer pressure, ignorant or angry adults, child abuse, predators, societal demands, or academic rigors, I can't fathom all of what it must feel like to be a child today.

But that's just it: your children are living it, day in and day out, with or without you. Be there for them, support them, nurture them, listen to them, and help them when you can but also help them know how to fight their own battles when they must.

## IF YOU'RE NOT TEACHING THEM TO SWIM, YOU'RE HELPING THEM TO DROWN

Independence isn't a gift or a luxury, it's a necessity. I liken it to those parents who endure a little crying and more than a few tantrums to teach their children to swim at an early age as opposed to those who keep turning away from the community pool, putting it off until later. I once overheard an older woman say to a first-time parent, "If you're not teaching them to swim, you're helping them to drown."

An old parable still holds true: "Give a man a fish and he eats for a day; teach him how to fish and he eats for life." Life with my mom meant a whole slew of life lessons. I think back now to how she meticulously explained *everything*!

Whether it was explaining the necessity of washing the germs off an apple (to guard against disease) or not starting the car with the garage door closed (to avoid carbon monoxide poisoning) or pointing a pressurized bottle away from the body (to avoid taking your eyes out) or not leaving items inside the can in which they were packaged (to avoid getting botulism), she was teaching us all the time. She did all that she knew how to help us swim!

This same truism can be applied to nearly every nook and cranny of your child's life. Seriously, you can take this same sentence, remove the words *swim* and *drown*, and fill in the blanks with much of what your child encounters in a single day.

Let's try it and see:

- "If you're not teaching them to *tie their own shoes*, you're helping them to *trip*."
- "If you're not teaching them to *do their own homework in grade school*, you're helping them to *fail when they get to junior high*."
- "If you're not teaching them to *pack their own lunch*, you're helping them to *be more dependent*."
- "If you're not teaching them to *be responsible for their own actions*, you're helping them to *dodge responsibility for everything they do later in life*."

Shoelaces, sack lunches, and homework—we could play this game until the cows come home! The point is that independence is so much more than a gift; it's literally a tool for survival.

## Ten Tips to Cultivate a More Independent Child

What would your child do in a situation without you, and could he or she live without you? No parent wants to think this way, but we all must.

There is no way on earth to be with your child every minute of every day in the long run. And thinking is just the beginning; we must act if we want to help our children achieve true independence before they need it, not after.

Here are ten ways to do just that:

**The First Tip:** *Start Small*

We're not talking about tossing your child into the deep end and watching her choke, sputter, and flail her way back to shore here! Children mature at different ages, and I've seen eight-year-olds who can not only pour milk over their own cereal before school every morning but pack a lunch before the bus gets there and, if necessary, whip up a frozen dinner if their mom's late getting home from work!

By the same token, I've seen ten-year-olds who have to be constantly reminded to tie their own shoes and brush their own teeth. Only you can decide how independent your child should be and how soon.

My only hope is that you recognize the importance of independence and begin to slowly help your child mature and grow through small, daily changes, such as

- making his or her own lunch;
- picking out his or her own clothes; or
- doing his or her own homework.

Depending on your child, you may already have worked this out or these could be considered Herculean tasks. Either way, you've got to start somewhere!

**The Second Tip:** *Now or Never*

There are things you can be doing right now, today, the minute you put down this book, to help your child become independent. No matter what time of day you're reading this, or where your child is on the developmental scale, you can begin to increase his or her independence immediately.

Take a look around you and see.

**The Third Tip:** *Cold Turkey's Too Much? Try Warm Turkey Instead!*

Not every kid will succeed in becoming independent "cold turkey." For instance, if you're one of those "helicopter parents" who hovers around your child all day long, this is going to be an adjustment for both of you!

So if your child making his or her own lunch is going to be a huge deal in your house (in the beginning it takes *forever*), start "warm turkey" instead. Have your child bag his or her own carrots or cut his or her own sandwich one morning and then make his or her own sandwich the next morning. It may take a week for your child to make his or her own lunch from bag to bread to peanut butter to carrot slices in a satisfactory way, but imagine what that week can teach him or her!

Let's apply the same "warm turkey" method to homework. Maybe your child is used to you checking every problem for him or her every night after school. Is this as independent as he or she can be? Shouldn't he or she be doing most of the work, if not all, by himself or herself?

Let's try weaning yourself away for a while. Even if you want to continue to spot-check and supervise your child's homework, you can say to your child, "Okay, I've helped you with problems one through sixteen. Now, you try to do problems seventeen through thirty-two yourself." This is a great way to provide the support your child wants while still providing him or her with the independence he or she needs. Eventually, he or she may not even need your help at all!

**The Fourth Tip:** *Partner for Success*

If you're not comfortable fighting this battle of independence alone, seek help from your other family members, friends, and neighbors.

Kids love to play one adult against the next. If Mom tells Little Jimmy to wash his own plate and put it in the dishwasher for the first time, you can bet before he even leaves the table Jimmy Jr. is going to be asking Jimmy Sr. if this is really completely necessary!

Discuss the need for more independence for your child and have a set strategy in place. It doesn't have to be anything too formal or rigid, just a tacit agreement that, "From now on, Jimmy is going to rinse his own dinner plate *and* put it in the dishwasher."

This way when that awkward moment comes at the dinner table and Jimmy is expecting Dad or Uncle or Auntie or an older brother or sister to have his back, you will all be on the same page.

It might be tough at first, but imagine how happy you'll be—and how proud he'll be—when Little Jimmy walks away from the table, rinses his plate, and successfully slides it in the dishwasher!

## The Fifth Tip: *Practice and Patience*

"Rome wasn't built in a day," my mother would often say, and you don't get to the top of Mount Everest by celebrating at the first base camp; you have to keep climbing! So it is with independence.

If the first goal is to rinse his plate, spend the time you need to make that happen. But the minute he masters that task, set another one, such as putting the dish in the dishwasher.

Have a schedule of goals. Give Little Jimmy a couple of days to master the dishwasher, a couple of more to clean the table, etc.

Forging independence is not an exact science. Be careful not to breed insecurity at the cost of attempting to instill independence since children progress at individual paces.

## The Sixth Tip: *Reward Accomplishments*

There's great value in rewarding success appropriately, the key word being *appropriately*. I'm not one to recommend sending Jimmy to Disney World just for clearing his plate, but it is perhaps worth

- an extra half hour of his favorite video game;
- an extra cookie for dessert;
- an extra bonus on his allowance; or
- one more hour of TV.

That's where the word *appropriate* comes in. Do what you feel is best and most effective when rewarding your child for reaching his or her goals. Be it a cookie, family time, computer time, or an extra half hour of free time before bed, celebrating achievements is one way to recognize goals' importance.

## The Seventh Tip: *Children Actually Desire Independence*

Sometimes the things children resist the most at first are the very ones they tend to be obsessed with and truly enjoy in the end! Have you ever taught a toddler to do something, and then later tried to do it for them? You will see him or her hollering and screaming to show you that it is his or her job to do. Or just watch a kid who goes kicking and screaming to his or her first bike-riding lesson, sans training wheels. Chances are two weeks later you'll be praying that he or she will take an interest in something else, anything else! You have to chase him or her down just to get him or her off the bike to grab a quick meal!

Independence is desirable! You just have to give it a shot.

### The Eighth Tip: *Failure* **Is** *an Option*

Not every kid is ready for every lesson the first time you give it to him or her. If Susie is too young or immature to do her science fair project all by herself, the experience could be so miserable that she'll never relate to science again.

Work with your dear little one to wean yourself off of her first independent project, but don't be afraid to help in an emergency.

Be patient, listen, and be alert for signs that you may have taken the training wheels off too soon. It's okay to put them back on; that's what screwdrivers are for!

### The Ninth Tip: *Baby Steps Move You Forward*

A dish here, a homework assignment there—it all adds up. Life moves in inches, not feet, and children learn by degrees, not right angles. Give your child time, give yourself time, and give each other a break!

You can't go from nurturer to drill instructor overnight, but you can gradually and effectively transition to a parent who expects more from your child, and just as naturally, your child will grow to expect more from himself or herself.

The trick is to start slow. Start small, but start; inch forward, but move. Baby steps are still progress, even if it takes a while to reach your destination. The key is to start the journey, no matter how long it takes.

### The Tenth Tip: *Try and Try Again*

"If at first you don't succeed," was a favorite saying of Mom's. Usually all she had to say was that much, the first part, and before long we would finish it with her "try and try again."

You don't need me to tell you that parenting isn't black and white, but predominantly a shade of gray. What works for your mother, your sister, your neighbor, or your aunt might not work for you.

Some kids are born seemingly ready to leave the nest while others take more time to find their wings. Either way is okay. Development happens; it's pretty much the only absolute in parenting! What we can't control is when it happens; all we can do is try to foster it.

And try ... and try some more. Keep trying. If Courtney is allowed to graduate to a new, more time-intensive hairstyle but is not diligent with the upkeep a week later, it's okay. But it shouldn't be too long before she is ready to show you an even better way to properly take care of her new style. Praise her for that. If "Little Jimmy" can put his own plate in the dishwasher this week, it shouldn't be too long before he's ready to make his own breakfast while you get ready for work. But if it takes him two weeks to learn the lesson, don't give up; hang in there and let him know how important this is.

They will get it eventually, and all that time you invested toward their independence will make your life and theirs better—in the short *and* long run.

## PARTING WORDS ABOUT MORE INDEPENDENCE SOONER

Life is full of watershed moments—your first kiss, your first child, her first word, his first steps. Parenting in particular has more than its share of "firsts." What is independence but more firsts?

Think of how proud you are with each new show of independence. You wouldn't think of robbing your child of those necessary developmental experiences, would you?

So why are you still doing his or her homework or tying his or her shoes?

## BENCHMARKS OF INDEPENDENCE

- Your role as a parent is to give your child the tools to enjoy freedom when it is time or it naturally happens.
- Gaining independence is a process. It will take some kids longer than others; be patient but persistent.
- Don't be afraid if some of your child's steps toward independence end in failure; failure *is* an option, but giving up isn't. Never give up!

# Chapter 8

## Love Your Sister

ACCORDING TO MY MOTHER, she and her only sister Ellen, or "Aunt Sister" as we called her, never had a fight—ever. I also know that my aunt often told her children the same thing. Who really knows?

Maybe they really did not have any disagreements, but more than likely it was that their disputes were so minor, so inconsequential, that they never stood out in their memories.

That sibling love, that bond between them, must have been something my mother wanted desperately for me and my sisters because from the beginning, my mother would have Fran and I hug and kiss each other, saying, "Love your sister."

Fran and I admittedly are pathologically close, no small thanks to my mom. The twin thing only magnified the fact that we were something more than sisters—we had the same imaginary friends and family as children (really!) and spoke to each other in a secret language (some, including our sister Joan say,until this day). We finish each other's sentences and thoughts. But all of us sisters check in with each other at least daily, and it all started with Mom.

"Love your sister," my mother would always say, in the biggest of times and the smallest of circumstances—in the grocery store after a minor sibling squabble, on Christmas Day gathered in front of the tree posing for photographs, after a rambunctious birthday party when all the guests had gone home or before a big family gathering when she knew we'd wind up roughhousing out of her sight, and oftentimes for no particular reason at all.

And we did. We heeded her words back then and we continue to heed them now. They were a constant reminder to us of the most important thing that matters in this world: love.

That's what being a sister, a daughter, a son, a brother, a mother, a father, an uncle, a dear friend, a grandparent, an aunt, a nephew, a niece, or a cousin is all about: love of family.

And for many in these modern times, family also may mean that there is no blood relationship at all, but there is the same genuine love and concern present in the household, whatever that household looks like.

*Fran and Me with our sister Joan*

*Aunt Ellen, my mother's only sister, and Mom at Mom's retirement celebration*

## THE MODERN FAMILY IS STILL A FAMILY

I've known many a nuclear family—mother, father, and two and a half children—who had as many issues as the rest, and many single-parent households that raised loving children with ease. However, I remember the ridicule aimed at me as a child when my parents divorced. It still perplexes me how adults are prone to judge children because of the actions of the adults in their lives.

"You know her father is a drug addict."

"You know she was adopted."

"Have you heard that he is not her *real* father?"

For me it was, "Your parents are getting a divorce!" I still remember the feeling I had when a childhood friend yelled that to me as if it meant that I had the plague. Thank God I had my mother, who never used that station in life as a crutch. Thank God she kept us out of the middle of the adult stuff.

So, regardless of who is at home or who you call family, as long as children are loved by some caring adult(s) and given proper guidance, this much is true: *they will thrive.* Given the makeup of single-parent homes, foster homes, same-sex-parent homes, divorced homes, adoptive homes, etc., it is imperative that guardians embrace the support of others when necessary.

I loathe the overused phrase "broken home." There is nothing broken if the love and desire to make it together is there. The key is to not raise children with broken spirits, broken dreams, or broken promises. Many of today's "modern" children are also being raised by or co-parented by grandparents, aunts, uncles, and siblings along with babysitters, teachers, and neighbors.

Family support is just that—support for a family when needed. As always with children, the key is to provide unconditional love and make a difference in their lives.

## EVERYONE NEEDS TO BELONG

By my way of definition, *family* is just another word for *belong.*

Kids know only this: where they belong. If the love is flowing, if their home is warm and inviting, if they are nurtured and appreciated, listened to and respected, disciplined and taught the rules, values, and life lessons, that is home, that is family, that is belonging.

Luther Vandross, the beloved and talented R & B singer, had it right when he sang, "A chair is still a chair, even when there is no one sitting there, but a chair is not a house, and a house is not a home, when there is no one there to hold you tight, and no one there, you can kiss good-night!"

Luther may have meant these words in a romantic sense, but the same holds true for children. And guess what? The adults who give them the greater sense of belonging, even if they are not parents, are the ones with whom kids will identify and to whom they will belong. That's why children need strong adult figures in their lives to fill the voids, or all kinds of negative belonging will take precedence. You have a captive audience with your child. Who better to be the best role model than you!

And, again, it doesn't matter if the home is filled with aunts and uncles, if Grandma makes their breakfast and Grandpa tucks them into bed at night, or if the home is a mansion, a trailer, a townhouse, or an apartment.

Home isn't just where the heart lives; it's where children belong to a working, functioning, eclectic family unit. Today's modern family doesn't necessarily look like the Cleaver household or *Little House on the Prairie* or even *The Cosby Show*—it may still for some children, but that certainly is no longer the norm, and it wasn't my norm growing up.

My mother was a hardworking single mother who did all she could to support her three daughters, but many times she had to call on others to help out in a pinch; they were all family as far as my sisters and I were concerned.

## BUILDING THE FAMILY FOUNDATION

More than just titles like "mother" and "father," families are cohesive units that help to build the foundation of a child's early life. That's where the emphasis needs to be—on the child, not on what the family looks like.

Don't worry if your family unit more closely resembles a patchwork quilt of loving, supportive blood relations, friends, neighbors, coworkers, or significant others. I have a dear great-nephew and a darling great-niece, and Fran and I have always played critical roles in their lives, emotionally and otherwise. I cannot imagine caring any more for biological children, and the investment in them is beneficial to all of us. "Auntie" and "Aunt Fran" are trusted members of their developmental team.

Trust me—children respond as much to those whom they view as family than those who traditionally should be. Responsible caregivers focus on making sure that no matter who is involved, they are there to provide a strong base of support and foundation on which your child can grow.

## BELIEFS START EARLY

Why is a strong foundation so important for children? Simply put, *beliefs start early*; very early. What your children learn at home from the people who are there, raising them, can improve, delay, inspire, or depress them for life.

So much of what we experience as adults—moods, temperaments, outlooks, prejudices, beliefs, and judgments as well as tolerance and understanding—is "installed" early on in life.

Teachers hear it all the time; when a child talks about which presidential candidate he or she is voting for or what he or she feels about a particular celebrity or social matter or race of people, that comes directly from what he or she has heard around the dinner table at home or riding in the car on the way home from school. What a powerful impact direct and immediate family members have on children no matter what that family looks like!

In fact, before early childhood education from a public or organized school enters the picture, family is a child's primary, most powerful, and often *only* influence of beliefs, values, judgments, rules, and lessons.

## EDUCATION IS INSPIRATION

Once school enters the picture—be it day care, preschool, or otherwise—a whole new family comes into the picture. These people—teachers, support staff, administrators, teacher's aides, counselors, and more—should all be considered a part of your family as well.

After all, teachers are basically surrogate parents for seven and a half hours every day! That's more than many actual parents spend with their children, and the influence they have on your child's early years is immense and immeasurable. It is well documented that students do better when parents are engaged in the educational process. The information flows both ways.

*Family picture at Mom's birthday (January 2011)*

The education at school is reinforced at home, and the teachers gain insight into the family's expectations at school. That is why parent-teacher conferences are crucial and why Parent Teacher Associations (PTAs) are so important.

Now, my mom didn't need a date predetermined by the school's calendar for a conference, an inquiry, or an update. We knew that, and the teachers knew that.

Be involved in your child's education, be there for registration, know where his or her homeroom or classroom is, meet his or her teachers, volunteer when and where you can, or at least make parent nights and meet-and-greets a priority. Be that parent who shows up when it counts and whom the teachers and school officials personally know. At school, you want to be present, not absent.

When teachers know more about you and how you relate to your child, it becomes easier for them to fit into the picture as a supportive member of your child's educational team.

School is what you and your child put into it, so take advantage of the many opportunities and organizations that exist there.

If there are after-school programs that seem more valuable, more educational, and richer than a day-care program you've been using, make that switch.

Even something as simple as encouraging your child to check books out of the library, join the computer club, or play a sport can not only add more support members to your growing "family," but can make education a priority from day one!

Make education a priority. According to America's Promise Alliance, only about half of this country's public school students receive a high school diploma! And statistics are worse for African American students who, in some major metropolitan cities like Philadelphia, New York, and Miami, fall well below the national average.

School starts in the home, not in a classroom. The more educational experiences are expected, the more they become routine. The more we make education a priority at home—getting kids up and fed and dressed on time, helping them with their homework—the better prepared and the better invested they are in an education that will serve them well their entire life.

That is in large part why, in addition to my traditional duties at court, I founded a truancy court. I saw a growing need to hold both children and their parents *accountable for school attendance and participation.* Parents were tending more and more to give in to the notion "I can't make him go," or give in to the convenience of sleeping in after being up half the night or staying home to babysit their siblings or for not having the latest fashions. All of these excuses throw education right out the door.

In a home where education isn't being made a priority by the responsible adults, who will make it a priority? Kids certainly aren't going to police themselves and go above and beyond to hit the alarm clock, get out of bed, and rush off to school if the parents are basically giving them a get-out-of-school-free card more days a week than not. (Well, not most kids, anyway!)

Education is a gift we can give our children that is not only free to one and all but can literally save their lives. School, grades, extracurricular sports, activities, clubs, organizations, friendships, bonds—these are tools our children can use to fashion a bright future instead of one that ends with them dropping out of school, out of hope, and out of life.

One of the greatest demonstrations of love is caring enough to make plans for a child to have a bright future through formal and informal education.

Both of my parents were educators, and I knew early on from their teachings that education was the great equalizer. I often joke that as far as I know, education is the only thing that they had in common, but a proper education was certainly something upon which they agreed.

*Mom in her classroom (Oscar Smith High School, 1989)*

## Don't Box the Father Out of Your Child's Life

Fathers are important to a child's growth and development, even if they're not part of your family. My own father wasn't a part of our family for long, as my parents divorced when I was seven years old. My father is further proof of what happens when children are not given the proper nurturing and emotional support when they are young. His own mother died when he was about three years old. His father raised seven children as a single father. All seven of those children went on to earn college degrees, and my grandfather himself graduated from college when he was close to seventy years old.

The education piece was exemplary, but I have heard stories of how emotionally unavailable and sometimes cruel my grandfather was to his children. I don't know this to be true, as my grandfather died when I was ten years old, and I only have pleasant memories of him. I have never talked to my father directly about this, but I can say that he has always seemed unable to emotionally connect in the way expected, so there may be some truth to those claims. However, I have always known that he was doing the best that he could, given the hand he had been dealt in life. What he lacked in the warm and fuzzy department, he tried to make up with his humor, his storytelling, and his historically documented accounts of every single activity we engaged in and by chronicling every accolade.

Newspaper articles, program bulletins, photographs, graduation announcements—you name it, he's got it when it comes to his children's activities. To his many associates, church members, fraternity brothers, and fellow educators, there is no greater source of pride than his girls. I think we always knew that.

There are fathers who want to play an active role in their children's lives, even if they are not the custodial parent. On the other hand, it can be difficult when the father of your children isn't a part of their lives or, worse, doesn't really want to be.

It can be harder still when he disregards his children because he doesn't want to be a part of *the mother's* life. In rejecting the mother, he rejects his children as well. But whenever there is an opportunity to embrace the father-child relationship, take advantage of it! Think of the children first. If their father wants to participate in their lives, let him. Mothers, whatever you think of your children's father, they need him. And Fathers, don't use the excuse of not being able to deal with the mother as the reason for not meeting your responsibility to your children.

Don't be the type of parent who runs your children's father down just because your personal feelings about him are harsh; think of the kids first and what they need to hear about their other parent. Remember, at some point in your life, he was the greatest thing since sliced bread; give your children the opportunity to see that side of him too.

Some men who aren't great husbands, lovers, or companions are actually quite good fathers. Let your children's father into their lives, if not for yourself, then for your children.

## PARTING WORDS FROM MY FAMILY TO YOURS

Love your children.
Love your parents.
Love your brothers.
Love your sisters.

Love your aunts and uncles, your nieces and nephews, your cousins and their cousins.

It's simple: no tips, tricks, steps, or strategies—just love each other.

Love your family, whether it's nuclear, single-parent, working-parent, modern, or otherwise. You don't need money or material things or even words to love your family; just love them and they'll know.

Kind words, good deeds, phone calls, and hugs at just the right time or anytime will show them what love means; love is universal, and no love is more universal than family love.

Don't worry about what your family looks like—nuclear, single, perfect (no such thing), pretty, ugly, functional, dysfunctional—it is unique unto itself. And it's yours forever, for better or worse, blood or no blood relation. The sooner you look around and realize that in the end family is all we have, the faster you'll run and embrace your own.

*Love your sister.*

## BENCHMARKS OF FAMILY

- Share with your children that no matter what your family may look like, it's never "broken."
- If you're separated, single, or divorced, don't make excuses for why you can't be a family.
- If you're divorced or separated, even if the split was far from amicable, shelter your child from that reality. Don't speak negatively about the child's other parent directly or indirectly to the child.
- Help your child to respect his or her elders and those family members who may not be local, such as distant cousins, aunts, uncles, and grandparents.
- Teach love of self and family at every opportunity.

*Chapter 9*

# Watch Out for the Trucks

I HAVE OFTEN BEEN perplexed by how it seems as if the parental protective gene has mutated over the last fifteen to twenty years. For some parents, that protective gene that once appeared instantly upon the birth of a child now seems to have gone the way of dial-up telephones and drive-in movies.

In many regards, the protective parent gene has been more than just altered, but it seems to be actually missing in a significant number of new, mostly young parents.

Just recently, while watching as much of the television broadcast of the Casey Anthony trial as I could stomach, I was reminded that what I had previously observed is, in fact, true. The fact that a prosecution could fashion as a strategy the idea that a mother preferred nightlife and partying over her child would clearly have been absurd at one time in our history, but no longer. Now it's a perfectly plausible and, to a significant portion of our population, a perfectly acceptable scenario.

What kind of parental protective gene am I talking about here? I'm talking about what I grew up observing in my own mother's house: that natural, intense, and undeniable throw-yourself-in-the-way-of-a-bus-to-protect-your-child instinct.

It was the way that my mother, until her last days of driving, would throw her arm across the front passenger seat to protect her children whenever she came to an abrupt halt while driving her automobile. It was that same protective gene that she had that alerted us not to tell her about a possible harm we might encounter, to save her from the anxiety and worry that would accompany such revelation. It was that mother wit that would have her call us out even when we tried to conceal certain dilemmas.

That was my mom. You had better not mess with her babies! That's why we learned as we got older to not even tell her about an unkind word someone may have spoken, or some misdeed done to us, because she held on to that. She didn't play with the notion that her children may have been mistreated or put in harm's way physically, mentally, emotionally, or otherwise.

For my sisters and me, this perspective made all the difference growing up. I sincerely can't imagine what my childhood, even my adulthood, would have been like without it.

The very idea that there was always someone willing to go to untold lengths to protect us served to make us feel more secure when we needed it the most. We knew undoubtedly that there was always, always someone who had us covered, not just riding in the car but in every other possible scenario as well. Even within the last few years, after my mother's difficulty with balance made it more difficult for her to walk without the risk of falling, she never lost that instinct. I was awakened by my doorbell ringing one evening to find her standing at my front door. She had to conquer the long walkway from the street up to my front door as well as negotiate two sets of steps to check on me. She said it was because I had not answered the phone, and she knew that I was not feeling well. She had driven herself over, even though she should not have been driving; otherwise, she would not have been able to sleep that night.

## WHEN DID "OVERPROTECTIVE" BECOME A BAD WORD?

In some ways, perhaps, we were overprotected since anyone who knew us knew that Puddin' was not going to let her children take too many chances without having all the details worked out in advance.

We were overprotected in the sense that we were not allowed to roam whenever and wherever we chose. I overheard a lady recently say to her teenage daughter, "I pick your friends." *Wow,* I thought, *that's what I'm talking about!* Even though Mom didn't literally pick our friends, our associations had to pass muster with her. She was careful and sensitive about the kind of influence our peers had. How I wish so many more would take the same approach. Since when did parents start letting the children dictate where they go and what they do after school, what they do on the weekends, and who they hang out with instead of the other way around?

Parents, if you learn anything in this chapter, in this entire book, let it be these three words: *protect your children*. Children who end up in the criminal justice system often get in trouble when they are supposedly spending time at a friend's house.

A fatal flaw occurs when the parents of the child fail to communicate with just who exactly his or her friends are, where they will be, and who will be supervising. "Spending time at a friend's house" can be code for doing just about anything the child wants to do, particularly if you take—or show—no interest in who your child's friends are.

That means that children are supposed to be somewhere when in fact they are not. That lack of checks and balances in your child's life affords him or her the opportunity to be unsupervised and ripe for legal transgressions and unsafe conduct.

Here are some situations that need to be sanctioned by parents before children even think about participating in them:

- sleepovers
- field trips
- studying at the public library
- outings to the mall
- concerts
- movies

The goal is not to create a police state in your own home, but merely the perception, understanding, and atmosphere that you are there to protect them. That is your role, and there is nothing wrong with it.

## THEY GROW UP SO FAST (OR DO THEY?)

Parents, it's dangerous out here! Your children are not equipped to know what is best for them—that's your job, that's your role, and that's what they need most from you.

While it's important to share good times, even friendship, with your children, your main role is not as their friend, buddy, pal, or cohort; it is to be their parent. They have enough friends.

Pave the safe path for them wherever they go, whether or not you can physically go with them. Obviously, it is impossible to always be with them, but it is pure negligence to allow children the liberty of deciding what and who is best for them until they are mature enough and old enough to make those choices for themselves.

It's often said that our children grow up too early these days, but that's far from the truth. They don't grow up too early at all, they simply grow wise—a better word may be *savvy*—in the ways of the world.

Thanks to the Internet, reality TV, and an unlimited stream of easily downloadable, scannable, and viewable information, children know far too much about the adult world than they could ever truly comprehend. Saying they are grown up is a misnomer because they only *seem* grown up. In fact, they have not actually matured.

While your children may look wise beyond their years, they aren't. They're simply tall, dressed-up children playing at being, or at least looking and sounding, grown up.

## "Watch Out for Trucks"

When Fran and I were about eight years old, we sat in the backseat of the car as our mom pulled up to the drive-thru window of her bank. We were anxiously awaiting the candy suckers that the bank teller dished out, but on this day the suckers came with a dose of advice. The teller handed them to us with the admonishment to "watch out for the trucks."

As we drove away from that window, we all immediately began to ponder what this teller meant by her odd, almost-cryptic statement. We all looked out into the oncoming traffic, wondering if perhaps the teller was trying to tell us something we couldn't quite see with our own eyes. There were no trucks visibly near us; we weren't even on a busy street.

Was there a particular truck she had in mind? Or did the word *truck* have a hidden meaning? This "watch out for the trucks" was the subject of discussion for many years to come. What in the world (another favorite expression of my mother's) did she mean by telling us to watch out for the trucks?

Although we never came up with an absolute conclusion, the phrase "watch out for the trucks" took on a life of its own in our family. A common departure from each other throughout our lives would end with "watch out for the trucks." When we anticipated a particularly daunting day, the warning would be to "watch out for the trucks." When we knew one of us would encounter a difficult colleague or a professional challenge, we finished with "watch out for the trucks!"

## PARTING WORDS ABOUT WATCHING OUT FOR THE TRUCKS

The real point of that bank teller's warning that day was simple: *be careful.* In all things, every day, in heavy traffic or on a quiet country road, "watch out for the trucks." Caution was not to be thrown to the wind. That phrase became a theme in our lives that still resonates.

The "trucks" could be a number of things:

- dangerous people
- strangers
- situations
- words
- language
- peer pressure
- relationships

The idea is not to be intimidated or discouraged to do new things, but rather a constant reminder to move forward cautiously, with both eyes open. "Watch out for the trucks" also suggested that we were to check in with each other so that we were always accounted for.

So what "trucks" are there in your child's life? And how can you best help your child to avoid them?

## BENCHMARKS OF PROTECTING CHILDREN

- It's simple: ask questions.
- Don't automatically accept the child's assessment of the situation as factual.
- Don't instill fear, but instead develop an attitude of readiness and preparedness.
- Always seek to know where your children are, whom they are with, and, when possible, be there with them.
- "Watch out for trucks" in all shapes, forms, and sizes.

# Chapter 10

## The *Endurance* Test

IF THERE'S ONE THING that is permanent within a family, it's the legacy that is left behind. It is common knowledge that we experience change daily; nothing really stays the same. Kids get older, go through phases, and find different interests. Today it's soccer or cheerleading, tomorrow it's downloading as much music as possible, and the following day it's an obsession with the video game *Call of Duty*, track and field, or pageants. Interspersed in there are the highs and lows and the pains of growing up.

As adults, we too experience changes and weather our ups and downs. We lose and gain jobs, buy and sell houses, and make and break friendships and marriages. Through it all, this much has always been true and will always be true: you will leave a legacy.

The question becomes what kind.

### ENDURANCE MATTERS

Many Americans don't give much thought to history these days. I always cringe when I see those "man on the street" clips on television where some comedian or newscaster asks random citizens pretty simple questions, such as, "Who was Thomas Jefferson?" or "What's the capital of Florida?" Most of us adults could use a refresher course in history.

It's not that we actually need the answers to theses questions to live our daily lives, but there are some historical facts that really do make a difference in the development of pride and character. Family history lessons are critically important. It is vital that we know about our family's past as well as our nation's past to fully appreciate the sacrifices past generations made to help us achieve our current goals.

To not know the history of our cultures or the relational issues that define our existence is fatal. To forget the sacrifices made by family members is not only disrespectful to those sacrifices but also tragic! To forget the sacrifices made by our military, community organizers and other leaders, inventors, writers, scientists, and mathematicians is to deny history and the events that molded our past. It is often said that those who do not know (or appreciate) their history are doomed to repeat it. In short, you must know where you have come from to know where you are going. That especially holds true in terms of reference points for children.

Part of raising children is helping them decide what's important in life, what *matters*, and what *endures*. Oftentimes what matters to us is what matters to our kids, because like so much else, the examples are demonstrated at home.

When I was growing up, parents would quiz their kids at the dinner table. History, politics, homework, whatever; dinnertime was a time for lively discussion, even debate. Now we eat in front of the TV, if we eat together at all.

I'm not saying that every moment needs to be a lesson, but I am saying that we must make teaching and understanding our past a priority. I think it's fitting as we close out our time together that I talk about the future and how important it is to focus on what matters: to you, your family, and your children in the long run.

## TIME: *THE GREATEST GIFT OF ALL*

What endures the most from my mother's life is her appreciation of time. She knew the value of a moment; how powerful it could be as a teacher imparting a lesson in front of her class, sneaking a glance between mother and a daughter, appreciating a good laugh, or relishing the time spent with good friends and family. And she wasted no time teaching life lessons.

No matter how busy our mother was, she gave freely of her time. We were her life and she was ours; she made that clear from day one. And even when she had to live her life—going to work, working two jobs, pulling duty as the ticket salesperson at her school's sporting events or on parent-teacher nights, or even spending a rare night out with friends—she never made us feel like we were any less than the center of attention. In fact, whenever possible, we were integrated somehow into those events.

So I know firsthand that whether you hardly have any time to give or even if you have nothing *but* time, you have so much to give to your child. Time is the one gift that truly endures, that truly matters, and that truly makes a difference in how our children grow.

I'm not saying that time is all it takes to raise a healthy, happy, productive child, but the gift of time is irreplaceable and invaluable. Once it is gone, you can never get it back!

## EIGHT TOOLS THAT HELP IN THE LONG RUN

What can we teach our children that will last? What lessons will endure? What habits, traits, or sensibilities can we share with them that will make them better, happier, smarter people?

Once again, I can only point to my mother's teachings to help me form this list. These are the lessons that have endured the most:

> **Spirituality:** From the very beginning, my mother told us how very special we were to her, and how she knew that we were her "gifts from God" (her words). We were raised based on spiritual principles and continually taught to look higher for guidance. Soul-searching was encouraged on a regular basis. We attended church service regularly with her for as far back as I can remember and therefore were also exposed to other spiritually based activities. We participated in the children's choir, ushering, church plays, vacation Bible school, church trips—you name it! Doing so was not optional. My mom didn't just tell us what to do, she incorporated it as a major component of our upbringing. The guiding principles were evident. Most importantly, she prayed over us often and taught us to pray—pray anywhere and often. You best believe I have done it—in bathroom stalls, in the stairwells at work, in elevators, while driving, and I know that my sisters do the same. That framework that she lived and established is clearly a gift that keeps on giving. It wasn't the religious rituals so much that have inspired me all these years, but my personal relationship with the Almighty Judge, based in large part on the early and constant foundation my mom laid

that is unmovable. More than anything, Puddin' led us to a belief system we could rely on for years to come. The point I am making is that parents have an obligation to teach their children moral and spiritual principles. A spiritual relationship can be cultivated at any time, but in my opinion, the window of opportunity is greatest when children are exposed early in life. I once attended a conference where some of the presenters were children who had been in foster care and spent a large portion of their childhood in transition from one placement to another. Surprisingly, many of the children said that what they missed most from not having a consistent home environment was the spiritual and religious teachings that more appropriately come from a loving parent. Even though they were being provided food, clothing, and shelter, they felt that what had been most neglected was spiritual guidance.

**Patience:** Teach your children patience. Let them know that good things may not necessarily come to those who wait, but that they do come (eventually) to those who work hard over a long period of time to achieve good things. My mom often proclaimed that "only the strong survive." In other words, there will be tests along the way, but the end result will be positive if we remain strong and steadfast. Patience truly is a virtue.

**Independence:** My mother taught us to be independent, to stand on our own two feet, but to never feel too strong to ask for help when needed. We knew early on to speak for ourselves and not get swallowed up by the crowd. The excuse that "everybody else was doing it" was never an acceptable explanation. Even with Fran and me, she recognized our individuality and our distinct value. She understood, recognized, and celebrated the need to be independent even from each other and for us to function as separate beings. She was always happy to see us demonstrate that independence, which allowed us to do things and go places!

**Humor:** A sense of humor is a gift that lasts forever. I can't really think of my mother without at least chuckling. We have enough inside jokes, hilarious situations, and unbelievably funny circumstances to last a lifetime. She taught us not to take ourselves so seriously as to think that we were the be-all and end-all. I am so grateful that we learned that it was all right to laugh at ourselves and with each other. I can remember so many occasions when we literally laughed until we cried. She also taught us to keep smiling and to always strive to make others smile as well.

**Perspective:** A proper sense of perspective can do wonders when children grow up to face an increasingly demanding, competitive, and often disappointing world. My mother would often assure us that it wasn't the end of the world when things went sour or that we needed to hold our heads high when others bashed us. She would remind us that no one could rob us of our dignity. She would also remind us that "Rome wasn't built in a day." In other words, slow down and take a deep breath when necessary. She would even sometimes say, "Take a little nap and then get up and start fresh." She encouraged us to tackle life in manageable pieces and keep things in proper perspective.

**Charity:** Lead by example and help your children understand the gift of giving. Even if you don't have a lot to give, children understand the concept of giving better when they see it in practice. I relish the fact that, to this day, I am a giver and not a taker. Takers suck the life out of givers at times, but I firmly believe that it is "more blessed to give than to receive." Translated, this literally means that when you give, you never have to worry about getting. There is an inexplicable joy that can only come through giving.

**Manners:** Teach your children manners. Knowing how to play well with others and handle themselves in social situations only adds to their human potential and value. Being respectful to others goes a long way (as discussed in chapter 6). As Puddin' used to say, "You catch more flies with honey than you do with vinegar."

**Humility:** Above all, teach your children that it's okay to be humble—that they don't always have to be the first, the greatest, or the richest. It's okay that our children aren't the *best* as long as they *do their best.* Taking such pressures off children at a young age ensures that they won't spend half their lives racing to catch up—or keep up—with those terrible Joneses!

## Parting Words about Endurance

I am grateful for the way my mother stressed both the future and the past while my sisters and I were growing up. We were not just taught to respect our elders; we were taught to respect the contributions they had made to our future.

So much of what I am grateful for about my mom is the way that she is such an integral part of my life even to this day; her wisdom, tutelage, sense of humor, and loyalty have a daily impact in my life.

Now that's true endurance!

So what impact have you had or will you have on your own child's life? What will he or she remember about you five, ten, fifteen, thirty years down the road? Will it be the fussing and the fighting, the tirades and the tantrums? Will it be that you were never there, or the empty promises and unrealized goals?

Or will it be the small things that you did to help your child grow up, trust himself or herself, and learn his or her gifts and treasures? Will it be the big lessons you taught with persistence and consistency?

The truth is that it doesn't take much to make a strong impression on a child. While the big things like graduations, birthdays, holiday presents, and anniversaries certainly stand out as some of our most powerful childhood memories, don't discount the small stuff.

What I remember most about my mother are the kind words she'd say when she didn't have to, or was busy. I remember the thoughtful touches, like remembering to sign my parent permission slips without me having to ask fifteen times or leaving a chocolate Easter bunny or pair of fun kneesocks on my bed, just because.

It can be intimidating to have your child's future in your hand, but from my own mother I learned that small things, daily, make a *big* impact now *and* later in life.

To give your child the gift of endurance, you simply have to start with the gift of your time … today.

## BENCHMARKS OF ENDURANCE

- Practice humility at home. Humble children learn to see life in perspective.
- If you want the lessons you teach to stand the test of time, begin spending more time with your child today.
- Give your child a sense of history. Go to historic landmarks, learn about the legacy in your own family, and learn from the past.

Help your child to become independent sooner rather than later. Independent children grow up a little sooner and are better able to endure some of life's toughest situations.

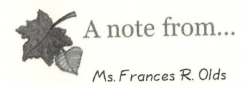

# A note from...

Ms. Frances R. Olds

My proudest accomplishments are my children: Joan, Eileen, and Francine. Being the mother of my children is my most outstanding achievement, and I'm humbled and blessed by their unceasing concern and loving care of me.

*A note from my mom*

## Epilogue

MY MOM TRANSITIONED FROM her earthly home to her heavenly home on February 13, 2011. Hers was a life well lived that impacted our lives and will continue to do so *forever*!

I didn't share this fact with you earlier because, for one, Mom passed while I was writing this book. Also because I didn't want you to dwell on her death—she never would have wanted that!

Even in this greatest loss, I see her smiling down on me, beaming with pride and nodding in approval that I have done another thing that I intended to accomplish. I really do have this tremendous urge to get her approval and share the trials and triumphs that went into producing this book, which I hope will be of benefit to many. Then I remember that she already approved, and she would be overjoyed that I am trying to help others to help "the little children" (a phrase we often used).

More importantly, I know that her teachings live on as if she's still alive. That's why the lessons in this book are so important to me and, I hope, to you; they are a living testament to the gifts my mother left behind.

In her own words, my mom felt that being the mother of her children was her "most outstanding achievement."

Shortly before she passed, Mom said, "Honesty, integrity, truthfulness, compassion, and self-worth were values I tried to instill in them. I can look back and say, 'God really does answer prayers.' Because Puddin' knew that I was writing this book, I had asked her to tell me in her own words what her goals were in raising us. She said I can look back and say, 'God really does answer prayers.' Yes, they have *gone far* and are ready for whatever else life has in store for them."

Thanks to Puddin', my sisters and I know the importance of being more than just good daughters, but the necessity of being good citizens as well. I think that's what Mom was really aiming for: children who could make the world a better place, no matter what they did.

I can still picture my mother in her deli uniform that one fateful summer and how she tried to do as well at her supermarket job as she did in teaching children the rest of the year. To me, that's the epitome of what being a good citizen is about: doing your part, no matter what role you have been handed to play.

In my work and in my life, and on my streets and in my city, I see this country's value systems deteriorating before my very eyes. In some small way, I hope that this book can help restore them. I'd like to thank my coauthor, my mother, for instilling in me the wisdom that informs these pages.

Really, it's an individual thing; everyone doing their part. If one reader does one thing to improve his or her relationship with a child and that child grows up to be a slightly better citizen, that reader sends a ripple through the world, as tiny as it may be. As Mom might say, "It may be just a 'drop in the bucket,' but a lot of little ripples make up a wave."

If your parents are still alive, reach out to them today, thank them, and share with them how much they mean to you. Then turn around and hug your kids. And then start being the kind of parent your kids will want to write a book about someday!